Here, There and Everywhere

Here, There and Everywhere

A British Soldier's Lot

by

FREDERICK MEMMOTT

The Pentland Press
Edinburgh – Cambridge – Durham – USA

First published in 1997 by
The Pentland Press Ltd
1 Hutton Close
South Church
Bishop Auckland
Durham

ISBN 1-85821-444-0

Typeset by Carnegie Publishing, 18 Maynard St, Preston
Printed and bound by Antony Rowe Ltd, Chippenham

Contents

1

My Early Years

My family consisted of my parents, one brother (George), two sisters (Joyce and Constance) and myself. We were originally from Sheffield but during my childhood, my father frequently moved about the country in order to keep in work and my mother, younger sister and myself accompanied him. My elder brother was married with a family and was working for EMI in Hayes. The elder sister worked in a shop. Altogether, I attended nine schools full time and three part time. In 1933, when I was thirteen, my father thought it was time for me to start earning some money and, initially, I got a job veneering furniture with a firm called Hymans. The family moved to Southall shortly afterwards and I was fortunate to be employed by EMI.

I first attempted to join the army in 1936, when I was sixteen years old, very unhappy at home and desperate to get away. The prospect of army life seemed exciting and an ideal means by which to escape. Unfortunately, the minimum age for entry at that time was eighteen. Another two years to wait was too long, I had waited long enough already. Without informing my parents of my intentions, I travelled to a recruiting office, told them I was eighteen and was accepted without having to produce a birth certificate or other proof of my age. I received the *Kings Shilling* payment on signing the enlistment papers as per the custom of the day. I was 'over the moon', but I should have consulted my horoscope!

After only a month's training at Aldershot, which I thoroughly enjoyed, my father discovered my whereabouts and immediately advised the authorities of my correct age. I, Frederick Memmott, was obliged to return home immediately and delay, for what seemed eternity, my rejoining the army. Others had got away with it, why not me? However, during the course of the following year, the age of entry requirement was reduced to seventeen. It was a welcome reprieve as far as I was concerned and I promptly took advantage by joining the Essex Regiment at Warley in Essex. This time there had been no need to lie about my age.

My reason for wanting to leave home at the earliest possible opportunity related to the attitude of my father whom I regarded as a tyrant. He was a blacksmith by trade and was also a very keen musician who could play a variety of brass instruments. A gold medallist, he frequently played in various bands and was determined I should also be able to perform to his standard. It was a case of tuition and practice to the exclusion of all other interests. Seldom was I allowed to take part in activities with other children. There is no doubt his teaching methods were first class. I became a competent player and at the age of eight I was playing in a junior band of the Salvation Army having learned the trombone, cornet and euphonium. By the time I was thirteen I was playing alongside my father in the Poolsbrook Prize Silver Band which was considered a great honour. Basically, this was a colliery band representing the four Markham pits in south Yorkshire and very highly regarded in the musical world. Eventually, it all became more than I could tolerate, hence the decision to become a soldier.

The training period in the Essex Regiment lasted six months. Most of my free time was spent in the gymnasium. Every evening, together with several friends, I worked on wall-bars and climbed ropes. Another interest was in shooting with both rifle and revolver. We were never idle and really enjoyed ourselves. Competition in the depot was keen and it definitely brought out the best in everyone. At the end of our training

I finished top in all the most important activities and, in gymnastics, broke all records scoring 129.5 points out of 130. The half point was lost for laughing at someone! On completion of our training we took part in summer exercises with the 2nd Battalion, which included a march to Colchester – a distance of sixty miles which took three days. Mock battles were fought and we fired blank shots when attacking or being attacked. Afterwards our weapons would have to be cleaned and oiled which, of course, took up valuable time in the evenings. You never saw the more experienced men carrying out this chore. They would only pretend to fire and keep the rounds in their pockets, saving their free time for other more interesting activities.

After Christmas 1937, the battalion learned it would be taking part in the Aldershot Tattoo of 1938 and intensive preparations started immediately. For a young soldier it was very exciting to have the opportunity to take part in such a professional show twice a day.

The Tattoo was very good and included a regiment of guards drilling several pipe bands with their drums and also the regiment of artillery on horseback who criss-crossed the arena at great speed with their gun-carriages. We gave a performance both in the afternoon and again in the evening. For each show we received twelve blue tickets; *blue lights* we called them. They were worth a penny each (in pre-decimal money) and they were used in the NAAFI to buy tea and cakes.

1939 arrived and it seemed we could soon be involved in another war. The battalion prepared for whatever might be in store. We dug trenches and more trenches. No one was in any doubt how to use a pick and shovel before we had finished. We could have done it in our sleep.

In August 1939 the battalion was on the rifle ranges at Purfleet when we received instructions to return to our barracks at Warley. Something was in the wind. Big *Ack-Ack* guns were appearing at many locations and we were responsible for delivering the ammunition. Our platoon went on guard duty at Bromley gasworks which was a welcome change from guarding our barracks.

2

The Phoney War

On Sunday 3 September 1939 we listened to the Prime Minister, Mr Neville Chamberlain, on the radio when he told the nation that Britain was at war with Germany. The air-raid sirens sounded as he finished speaking. We thought this was the start of hostilities – the real thing – and for the next few days the barracks were in turmoil with the preparations to fight a full-scale war. Lorries were loaded, weapons checked and re-checked and personal kit carefully examined to ensure no man went to war without his socks or a spare pair of bootlaces. We really enjoyed this period.

The following Wednesday we joined a train at Brentwood. First we went north, nearly as far as Manchester, then south to Bedford. This diversion, I believed, was to fool the enemy but it may have been a 'lash-up'. We were never to discover the true reason. Caution in everything was necessary during the war and government posters of the time carried the slogan *Be Like Dad, Keep Mum*. Finally, we arrived at the port of Avonmouth where we joined a waiting ship. "Don't get too comfortable," we were told, "you are only going across the English Channel." In the evening we started our crossing and we lay on the boat's deck having been given strict instructions not to talk or smoke. Even a cough was not permitted without obtaining prior authority.

The battalion disembarked at Calais and there joined a French train that was to take us to Brest. In normal times this journey would take a long time. We were solidly packed into the carriages and movement about the train was very difficult.

The train was shunted here, there and everywhere and we came to the conclusion that French trains were fitted with square wheels.

In Brest there were several battalions of British infantry stationed and there was a lot of rivalry and ill-feeling among the men. At the weekends, pickets were formed, with as many as 300 in one picket, to make sure all soldiers of the various units behaved themselves. Weekends were very lively indeed.

Part of our job in Brest was to guard the docks. I was on duty one day, patrolling along the quayside, when one of the ships in the harbour caught fire. It was about a quarter of a mile away from the quay and was heavily ablaze in seconds. Suddenly there was an enormous explosion and parts of one side of the ship landed about a hundred yards away from us. The metal made a considerable noise as it hit the quayside. We could not touch the debris because of the intense heat. It was an ammunition ship.

Our stay in Brest lasted for about two months before we moved up to the Lille area. We were transported in trucks that were in a dilapidated condition. They were labelled *10 horses or 40 men!* As I lay on the floor in a corner of the wagon I had a good view in the moonlight of an axle and a big wheel. The journey in these vehicles lasted three days and nights. We washed and ate by the railside – somewhere in France. Accompanying the convoy was a huge tanker on wheels with taps all round from which we filled our mess-tins with soup – it tasted marvellous.

We went on to our next billet in a village called Ganchon Le Gal. Very few of us got any sleep the first night as we all had the runs. Being taken short halfway across a field caused a bit of a laugh.

Our first guard duty in this area was on the gates of the local chateau below the servants' quarters. By this time I was a corporal and I was changing the guard at 6 a.m. one morning when the bedroom window above us opened and we all got soaked with the contents of a chamber pot. When I went to complain a young lady opened the door with nothing on. I was flabbergasted and made a hasty retreat. In France, we found out, there was a time and a place for everything but it was not necessarily the right place or the most convenient time.

During the phoney war, waiting for some action, the battalion carried out road repairs. It was exercise and we had many laughs with the locals. On wet days we were given a tot of rum when we arrived back at our billets. A so-called anti-tank ditch was also being dug covering many miles in length. I thought it was useless but nevertheless orders are orders! Each weekend saw several *passion wagons* going to Lille and Arras. I noticed the occupants were mainly married men and was told the places visited had ceilings lined with mirrors! Otherwise life was quiet and leave back home was being granted – my ten days were due to start in February 1940. The weather was awful both in France and in Britain. Our company was billeted in a dance hall and we slept on straw mattresses laid on the floor. Some of the men placed bottles of beer under their pillow and the following morning the contents were frozen solid. How any form of transport moved I do not know – the roads were of solid ice. When I packed my gear to go on leave it was snowing heavily and I had doubts about reaching the port from where I was to catch the cross-channel steamer. Somehow I did and arrived in a cold and snow-covered Sheffield the following night. All the family were pleased to see me, even my father, and after a very good leave they came to see me off at Sheffield railway station.

Following my return to France we were marching one morning in the teeming rain, with groundsheets around our shoulders, and reached a main road in the middle of nowhere. Five or six cars tore past – it was someone from the royal family. We were still hip, hip, hooraying when the cars must have been miles away. It was still raining when we returned to our billets at teatime having covered approximately twenty miles. Men needed the exercise regardless of the weather in order to keep fit for fighting when the time came for action.

3

The Real Thing

May 1940 came and, at last, the beginning of real action. We were all ready to meet the Germans and give them hell.

The battalion moved to Belgium and the Louvrain. My section was equipped with two Bren guns and one Boyes anti-tank rifle. We were good shots with the Boyes weapon but unless it was held correctly the result was either a broken jaw or an out-of-joint shoulder. Our officers had told us that German tanks were made of wood and we were looking forward to the opportunity of having a go at these armaments. What a shock we got! We were entrenched on a hillside ready for the attack. When the onslaught came, we fired long, hard and often but had no effect on the tanks. Had we not been halfway up a hill we would have been overrun. The Germans then went round us and we were forced to pull back. As we were fighting to get out the cry went out, 'every man for himself', which meant pull out and reform later. At the inquest afterwards, we were blamed for letting *wooden tanks* flatten us.[1] Presumably they were made of very hard hardwood!

As we continued through the hilly Belgium countryside we found the villagers had removed the handles from their water pumps. Like our fathers in the 1914–18 war we went for long periods without water. We lived on what could be scrounged.

---

1 Even as late as Christmas 1944, we were having difficulty destroying this type of tank – the heavily plated Panther Mark 4 with the powerful Piat rocket. The Boyes rifle was taken out of service as a direct result.

I ate sardines and, by way of a change, more sardines. At night, as we marched through the hills, we could see several towns ablaze.

My platoon was guarding our position one night when we saw German paratroopers landing. We were instructed to capture them and bring them in for questioning. A couple of us grabbed one who was about six feet, six inches tall and built like a bull. An officer took charge but could not get him to answer any questions. We were ordered to make him talk – something I had never done before. The two of us took turns to thump him with our rifle butts. Unfortunately, we went too far and he was incapable of talking. The officer gave me absolute hell. The next prisoner we brought in we merely handed over and then made ourselves very scarce, very quickly. He could do his own dirty work this time!

Another job we were given was checking refugees, as it was known, German soldiers were coming into our area dressed as women. Six men and I were stationed at one end of a bridge with the order to establish that female refugees really were women and not merely dressed as females. A cart arrived containing several refugees and I had my orders . . . and a problem. I was a well-brought-up lad with a religious background and a high respect for all women. How was I to find out their true sex? Frankly, I did not know one end of a woman from the other. I could not strip them nor ask them to strip. After much thought I came to a decision: I lined up the women and told them to take off their pants and lift up their dresses when I gave the order. Screeching and giggling, they did so. There were no men in that particular group. The local population looked on: the old women laughed – the old men sat with their faces set. They were surprised when I allowed the refugees to continue with their journey. I think the men thought we were intent on raping the young girls. After the experience I was a much wiser young lad.

Under attack from the Jerries, we were firing Bren guns through the night and inflicted heavy damage. The next day a fresh supply of ammunition was urgently needed and I was among the volunteers for the collection from the supply point. Passing through a village nearby I saw hundreds of French soldiers, led by an officer on horseback, going into a field and sitting down. They were waiting to surrender! There we were, fighting; behind us, the French, surrendering. After a couple of days we had to withdraw. As we did so we passed masses of abandoned French tanks in ditches. They were undamaged. An attempt was made to start some of them without success. Jerry was miles away! A German spotter plane flew overhead every day. There was no chance the French could shoot it down. Their gun crews were drunk and fired in the opposite direction.

As we came back through Belgium we fought on a canal bank for two or three days until Jerry broke through at a point further down the canal. Whether he went through the French or Belgian positions made no difference, we were obliged to retreat to keep the fighting line as straight as possible. We passed numerous RASC trucks which had been left in haste. They were hardly damaged. We made sure they were of no use to the Germans. Later, orders were given not to use any more hand grenades for this purpose – they would be needed for our own protection very soon. Jerry had surrounded us. We resorted to collecting French and German grenades and these were used to booby-trap other trucks we came across during our withdrawal. Just how many of our enemies were blown up by their own grenades when they opened a door or lifted the hood of a vehicle, I often wonder.

During the retreat we came across several guns of the Royal Artillery with split barrels. The reason for their abandonment was unclear, but it would have been difficult to tow them away with the roads being packed with refugees. The refugees constantly caused problems for us and we often had to cut across fields to reach our next position.

At each new location we would think we had the advantage when a breakthrough would occur and we would be surrounded. Our orders were to fight to the last man or the last round of ammunition. In the middle of giving Jerry considerable stick we would find him all round us and the order 'every man for himself' would be issued. Seemingly he was everywhere. Somehow Bill and I managed to extricate ourselves but, sadly, not everyone survived. This situation was to be repeated at frequent intervals. We retreated over muddy fields while being shelled, dived into ditches full of water and tried to keep smiling although our appearance was terrible. One of my best nights was spent in a field in the pouring rain and under shellfire, laid under some big rhubarb plants. I kept dry and slept like a log. On one particular day, I remember very well, we were enjoying the sunshine and holding back a German advance when suddenly everything went quiet. 'The bugger has gone behind us', we said. He had. You could not trust anybody. Again it was 'every man for himself'. Life was far from easy but it did not help to become depressed – we just soldiered on.

During the fighting near the Le Baseau Canal, French Senegalese soldiers stole our breakfast while we were engaged in other activities. The language we used was, and still is, unprintable. We went hungry and vowed our revenge. On another occasion, when being subjected to continuous shelling, machine-gunning and bombing we were obliged to retreat yet again. This time we managed to reach a barn for a breather and a French farmer supplied us with a drink and food, for which we were extremely grateful. As we rested he suddenly spotted a group of Germans heading towards the farm. Quickly he opened a trapdoor revealing a cellar packed with turnips. There was just enough room for my mate and myself to hide.

We laid our rifles on the opening ready to shoot if necessary. A German did try to get in but the smell of rotting turnips was too much for him and he departed. We were extremely lucky and so was that particular German. When we struggled out much later we could hardly breathe.

We had been out of the cellar only a few minutes when we heard a woman shout, *'je ne comprend pas'*. A German officer stood up in a big staff car with his men around him. It was back to the stinking hole in double-quick time. I was sure our time on earth would shortly be over but God is good and I have a big nose. After a while we came out, said goodbye to the farmer and set about getting back to our battalion.

In the evening we found another farm near our battalion. From a barn we set up our anti-tank rifle in a position where we could cover a bridge over a small river. The Germans regularly used motorcycles and sidecars and the Boyes rifle was excellent for knocking these vehicles out. After two days of fighting we moved out in the late afternoon. We had marched down a road for about three miles when I realised the lads had forgotten to bring the ammunition we had remaining from the barn. I decided to go back and fetch it. As I approached the farm German soldiers were moving in. It was dusk, my fatigue hat looked similar to those worn by the Germans and so I thought I would chance my luck. I walked through the gate at the same time as a truck was driving into the compound. I waved and continued to the barn. Men were moving about carrying equipment and making themselves comfortable. In the barn I found the ammunition, slung it over my shoulder and casually walked away. At the gate I stood with some enemy soldiers who were laughing at one of their men who had fallen in some manure. No one said anything as I walked out of the gate and down the road. I got back to my battalion early the following morning.

And so it went on, fighting, pulling out, fighting, pulling out and the same again, all to keep a straight fighting line. Men were given orders and the power to take over command should the situation arose. In every unit there was someone who could kill pigs or chickens and milk cows. I tried it only once – there was blood all over everyone and everything. Sardines were less of a problem.

Our battalion had gone into a little village called Le Guerre where we had a reasonable meal and a good night's rest. The next morning, the NCOs reported to our temporary orderly room for the day's orders. We were amazed to find all of our officers except one had vanished. It was unbelievable.[2] The battalion marched away from the village and had covered about a mile when twenty or thirty German Stuka aeroplanes flew overhead. We watched as they bombed the village we had recently left. Having caused much damage, the planes returned and turned their machine guns on us: we sustained several casualties. The villagers had moved away some time previously.

After many more similar incidents, we finally arrived at Watton. Fighting was fierce nearby and we needed to rest. We went into a house that was only a shell, laid down with some old curtains among the rubble and slept soundly. When you are young you can sleep anywhere.

At one time we were fighting alongside the Moroccans who were much better than the Senegalese. They would not stand any nonsense from German prisoners and would thump them when necessary and sometimes when not.

German paratroopers landed one night and our troops who were in vehicles manning radio sets received instructions to batten down and expect trouble. A friend of mine was in one

---

2 We later found out that these officers together with several of the more senior NCOs had instructed a driver to take them to Boulogne in a 15cwt truck. The driver was then told to make his way back to the men who were still fighting.

vehicle and I walked up and casually removed its cover. A rifle blasted near my face. The rifle had been rigged to go off if the vehicle was attacked. I was lucky, much wiser and never again did I make the same mistake.

The battalion was frequently attacked by the versatile Stuka aircraft. Nearly every day we saw them in four or five groups of twenty or thirty planes. They would be high in the sky, then come diving down at great speed and strafe their target with machine guns. Providing you were in or near a building they did not cause too much concern. We would walk around the farmhouse and be protected by the stone walls. Part of our equipment was a portable air-raid siren which, to be effective, had to be operated in an open field. Usually the men on alarm duty were the only ones above ground level during an attack and, consequently, the job was taken in turns. The Stukas prowled the skies and attacked whatever and whenever it suited them. During one raid the Stukas were machine-gunning while flying at treetop height and I clearly remember seeing the pilots racing past laughing their heads off. There was a black-headed fellow without a hat and wearing a black flying jacket roaring with laughter. He was having a great time. I tried to catch him with a Bren gun but failed. Were those pilots still laughing in 1944 when it was their turn to be chased, I wonder? We were so accustomed to seeing these planes that we could recognise the size and number of the bombs they carried – either two of 500 pounds or four of 250 pounds. A Stuka would drop two bombs and if the pilot did not veer off we would immediately take cover, knowing there were two more to be delivered.

In some villages we were leaving it was our job to set booby traps. We did not have training for this work but quickly learnt the techniques and after a few days we achieved a fair degree of expertise.

On 4 June 1940, my twentieth birthday, we assembled into RASC trucks which were to take us near to where our troops were engaged in fighting. It was a pleasant change from using our feet. We were enjoying the ride and singing away when we came under shellfire. I remember having got as far as *'rats as big as cats in the quartermaster's store'*, then . . . nothing. I came round under a hedge in a field feeling very groggy and saw a man looking at several dead bodies lying in a heap. Somehow, I managed to shout and he heard me. As he approached I saw it was my mate, Bill Syme. Both of us had landed in a hedge and had not been injured too seriously. At first I thought my right arm was missing. I wondered what my Mum would say. Bill helped me to sit up and my arm swung out. I quickly recovered and thanked the Lord that I had survived in one piece. Shortly afterwards I became acting platoon sergeant.

We headed northwards. It was strange experience. We passed many who were dead and said a little prayer and thought, 'there but for the grace of God!' Seemingly, every living person had vanished from the face of the earth – no British, no Germans and no locals. Retreating, as we were, and heading towards Dunkirk we met up with a few men who had been separated from their regiments. They formed into a platoon, I took charge and we continued on our way. We found a number of abandoned weapons which were in good condition and decided to take as many as possible with us.

On reaching the outskirts of Dunkirk, we were accosted by a French officer who decided to combine my men with his Senegalese soldiers. My previous experience of the Senegalese was that they were away like rabbits on the firing of the first shot. I refused to place my men's lives at risk through becoming in any way involved with them. Gesturing and swearing he stuck a revolver in my face and said he would shoot unless I obeyed his orders. I instructed my men to shoot him if he carried out his threat. My ploy worked but I did not feel completely safe until we were about fifty yards away. From that distance he would have to be an expert to hit me.

Dunkirk itself was deserted. We saw no one until we reached the seafront. There was shelling and bombing to which we had become accustomed. We boarded a destroyer, the *Greyhound*, and Bill and I headed for the 'sharp end' believing that would be the last part to sink, giving us more chance of survival. We settled down, set up our Bren gun and as we did so noticed a Stuka diving towards the ship. Four bombs were dropped; one landed on the ship and the others in the water nearby. The mechanism for ejecting depth charges was immobilised as a direct result of the raid. The ship appeared to sink slightly in the water but managed to leave the jetty and steam away slowly. A short time after leaving Dunkirk we encountered submarine activity. A young naval officer came down from the bridge. He looked at the depth charges on the deck which were about six feet long and four feet high. Tremendous things, they were! He decided we would manually roll them over the side of the ship and set the fuses so as to go off under the surface. We took down the ship's railings and every available man on board helped to get the charge over the side. It took a while to go over but had only just done so when it exploded directly underneath. The ship was savagely shaken and we landlubbers were convinced it was about to sink. The naval officer returned to the bridge to report. We conferred and it was decided, unanimously, that should he require another one shoving over, he could bloody well do the pushing himself. If we were going to sink, Jerry would do the honours – not ourselves. He came back and gave orders for another to be manhandled. We all, conveniently, went deaf. His face went purple.

The remainder of the trip was without incident and we arrived at Dover harbour where we disembarked. We wended our way to the waiting trains where we joined a lengthy queue and were given a cup of tea, an apple, an orange and a bar of chocolate. All that was needed was a new penny and it would have been like Christmas when we were kids.

When Bill and I were on the train, I thanked the lads with whom we had marched into Dunkirk. I was well pleased with them, they had never questioned my orders and all had come back with their weapons. My pal had his Bren gun and I had my Boyes rifle. We had marched into Dunkirk as a fighting platoon. It was something of which I was very proud. The officers who deserted us were another matter!

So much happened in a very short time and everything and everyone completely changed.

4

An Unhappy Return to England

When we boarded the train at Dover railway station, we had not the slightest idea to where we were being taken. The one we got on finished up at Tidworth where we spent the night under the stars in the local park. On the day following everyone was allowed to sign for £1 and go into the town for a drink or two. A pleasant change. We then moved into tents for the next four days.

One morning we were paraded and informed of the arrangements for rejoining our various units. Bill Syme and I would first travel to Manchester before going on to Knutsford. As we walked into our temporary camp, situated in the local park, we noticed our officers – the ones who had done a vanishing act in France – sitting at tables waiting to greet the men. My mate and I walked straight past, not even looking in their direction. For our insolence we were made to suffer. No one ignores an officer in the regular army, however justified. Many men had promised to do all manner of things at the time when we were left to fend for ourselves in France. Very few fulfilled their threats. Bill and myself both reverted to 'Private' the next day.

The battalion moved to Wales where we went under canvas and underwent further military training. All noncommissioned officers, from acting unpaid lance-corporals to the regimental sergeant major, found fault with us at every opportunity. It gradually dawned on us that instructions had been issued to give us the hardest time possible. Bill and I spent more time in the regimental jail than outside. It all got a bit much – to say the least. On one occasion we were put into the regimental

19

police compound which was surrounded with barbed wire and contained two four-man tents. The gate was secured with a thick chain and a huge lock. Early one morning I unlocked and opened the gate, laying the chain on the ground across the opening. I returned to my bed and awaited reveille. The regimental police thought we had gone away somewhere and dashed around the compound shouting and yelling. It must have been all of twenty minutes before one of them opened the tent flaps and found us. They were annoyed and did not take kindly to being made laughing stocks. Neither forgiving nor forgetting, they made sure we were punished and Bill and I were placed on bread and water rations for three days.

Bill and I were the regimental signallers and our platoon was near enough for us to pass a message by semaphore. The cookhouse was conveniently close to the camp entrance and the lads made sure we did not go hungry. They would regularly push plates of food under the barbed wire at the back of the compound. Thanks to them we ate very well. When the regimental police brought the dry bread and two bowls of water we usually kicked it away, thereby gaining the reputation of being tough guys.

At the end of September 1940, the battalion moved to winter quarters in a nearby town. Bill and I were on short pay until the end of November. We both drew two shillings and sixpence per week which was barely enough to buy Blanco for our equipment, Brasso for our buttons and Blacking for our boots. We relied on our good mates for a smoke – usually a Woodbine.

The sergeant of our platoon made life difficult and would continually find fault. It reached the point that I could not stand it any longer. One evening, when we were in a pub, I took him outside and gave him a good thumping. Later, I realised I was in real trouble and decided to go absent. Bill came with me. We were picked up in Newark after a few days and taken to the local barracks. The room in which we were confined was not very secure but being next to the guardroom it was not easy for prisoners to get out. In the evenings we were allowed to send out for supper if we could afford to and, at the time, we had money and enjoyed the occasional treat.

A Canadian was also detained with us. He had long fingers and was able to work them through a small hole in the door and undo the bolt on the other side. When the guard had fallen asleep, he would open the door and help himself to food from the kitchen. We also took advantage of the situation. It was hilarious to listen to the guards arguing over their missing supper.

On visits to the toilets we were accompanied by an armed guard. The cubicle door would be left open and they would hold the rifle with the bayonet about six inches from our chests. With our training we would have had no difficulty in overpowering them but they had been in the army only about three months and did not know any better.

During our long periods in detention, for want of something better to do, we used to hack the mortar out of the window jambs. We had no wish to escape: it was reasonably comfortable in there – though a little tedious. One morning a squad was drilling on the square which our window overlooked. As they marched up and down we made various sarcastic comments and criticisms. They halted and were facing us when the whole window fell out. The officers and the NCOs went berserk and our feet did not touch the ground. Later that day we were on the way back to our unit.

The court martial which was held about two weeks later sentenced us to a six month period in Shepton Mallet prison. We arrived at the prison in the early hours of the morning. As we approached in the half light it looked an awful place with its forbidding turrets. I thought to myself there will not be much to laugh at here.

On entering the prison we were stripped and searched by the civilian warders. Bill and I had not had a smoke for several days and we had made sure there was nothing whatsoever in our pockets. However, the prison staff found four cigarette ends in our clothing and accused us of trying to smuggle them in. Our protests were countered with physical and verbal abuse. I was about to retaliate when I remembered the advice of an old soldier, 'Keep your trap shut and serve your sentence'. This I did.

Life in prison was tough. Indignity was piled on top of indignity. We were chased around the prison courtyard with all of our kit wrapped in a blanket, into another building, down a long corridor with a cell doorway every two or three yards. At each door opening a member of the staff would stand holding a twisted webbing belt to hit you as you were chased into a cell. The staff would have a good laugh as we collapsed on the floor – for us it was not at all funny. Our blankets and our beds had to be laid out in a special way and inspected before we could have breakfast, or *Skilley* as it was called. The taste was dreadful and you had to starve for about a week before you could stomach the stuff. I was put into a cell with two other men who had been in prison for some time. They ate my food until I too was starving and had no choice but to eat it myself. There were either three men in a cell or one man on his own. At no time could you associate with anyone from your own regiment except in special circumstances. On the first morning Bill and I paraded side by side and were threatened with dire consequences if we did the same thing again.

With the movement of prisoners to and from the prison, there were opportunities for doing odd jobs – previous experience not being essential. I became the prison barber. All my hair had been cut off and the staff thought everyone should look the same. I did not keep that job very long due to not being too careful with a cut-throat razor which I was using for the first time in my life: one chap swore blind it was his ears I was after. At least it brought a smile to some faces.

One gets very sharp when in prison. When detailed as mess orderlies we collected food from the kitchen. Sometimes there would be about five hundred pieces of cheese on trays and I would eat the largest bits for myself before delivering them to the other inmates. At lunchtime we had a can with a round lid which held a sweet – always rice. We were constantly hungry and would mix the main course – always stew – with the rice. Following lunch we assembled near the kitchens ready for drilling on the square and mess-cans would be placed on the ground for later collection. The food which the recent arrivals could not eat was taken and eaten as we doubled around the yard. I once crammed two large potatoes into my mouth and the result was a skinned and bleeding mouth.

Officially, smoking was not permitted in Shepton Mallet prison and there were no means of getting cigarettes from outside. This problem was overcome by the use of rough brown toilet paper and nap taken off a blanket. All soldiers carried a field dressing which contained a white fabric gauze. This material would be lit by striking a thickish needle on the floor. It would soon begin to smoulder and in five minutes would be alight. The first time I saw this done was by a couple of chaps from Birmingham, one of whom had been in jail in civvy street. I met them when I was moved to their cell and helped them to get a smoke by waving a blanket. My new companions were in their thirties and both were in the Pioneer Corps – they were the only exceptions to the association regulation during my stay and this was because they came from different units. One was about six feet, six inches tall and had to bend to get through the door. The other was shorter and could neither read nor write. When he wanted to write home to his wife he would discuss with his mate what he wanted to say and how it would be written. These were long sessions and included some extremely personal matters such as how he missed her and longed for the day when they would be together again, etc., although expressed in explicit language. I felt awful having to listen to their conversations but to them it seemed so natural to be completely frank and open. He clearly missed his children and would ask his friend to write something like, 'Remember to get the kids some new shoes as winter is coming on'. I was sorry to leave them when the warders moved me to yet another cell. Shortly afterwards, I resumed my job as the prison barber. Some of the warders wanted me to cut their hair. I enjoyed the opportunity and became quite nifty with the razor.

Prisoners were allowed to go to the toilets, which were in the prison yard, only at specified times. If you were desperate, you were officially given one and a half minutes to deal with the problem. As soon as you had dropped your pants the warders would be bellowing at you to finish – an order which had to be obeyed whatever your circumstances. When the urinal was needed it was a case of running along a thirty-yard-long trough; you had to be finished by the time you got to the end or receive a heavy blow across the shoulders from a cane.

Life was not easy and if anyone dared to make the slightest objection or complaint they were placed on a *special*. Three or four burly warders would put you in a cell, leave you to ponder and return later to beat you up. I know, I tried it and the scars remain until this day. My nose is rather shapeless as a result.

Shepton Mallet is a very old prison; the cell floors are very uneven due to the continual pacing of a stream of prisoners, many of whom would have been wishing their lives away. Physical training was carried out every morning in a gravel courtyard even in the winter time. Your hands suffered alarmingly when there was a frost. The prison had no heating of any kind and in the winter it was dreadful. With nowhere to go we did exercises in our cells and tried to overcome the intense cold. Our beds were makeshift arrangements and none too comfortable. We were provided with three blankets – one to lie on, two to cover. It was not much to keep out the cold and we resorted to putting our clothes between the blankets. The next morning we had to replace them back in our kitbags for inspection. It was quite a job each day. Each evening prisoners were paraded and handed metal tins and plates which were rusted. By the following morning, when they had to be handed back, you were required to have polished them so that you could clearly see your face. When returned the warders would immediately throw them into a bath for further rusting before again handing them out at night. Many times we spent until lights out trying to get them polished to pass the inspection.

The prison had an execution cell which was used for its original purpose by the Americans during the war when they took it over. The head warder's house overlooked the private cemetery in the prison yard. That part was not used when I was an inmate but along with several others I helped to whitewash the execution cell and the shaft below. It was an eerie experience.

Sometimes during our afternoons in the prison yard, one or two of the younger warders would fancy their chances at a little unarmed combat. Many men could have dealt with them quickly and easily but it was not wise to take advantage. On one occasion a warder was wielding a big heavy cane and said I had to pretend it was a rifle. I was not at all keen to get involved but he hit me and I grabbed the stick, went over on my back and threw him across the yard. I got up first and placed my boot on his crotch and pressed a little. The other warders were watching and, not eager to have my stay extended, I pretended not to have done so well and went into a roll, out of the way. As he marched us off he thanked me for not completing the attack. We often gave lessons in unarmed combat afterwards.

Probably as a reward for not going too far in the prison yard, I was placed on a detail of three men for the relatively easy job, by prison standards, of cleaning and polishing the warders' rest room and eating quarters. We tackled the work with enthusiasm and were praised by the head warder. From then on it was our job. Occasionally, the warders would let us have some better food including cakes. Even the odd cigarette would be left out for us. We were under strict instructions not to say anything to anyone about these perks.

Each evening around 9 o'clock, a prisoner in one of the cells above would sing for about half an hour. He had an excellent voice and it could be heard throughout the prison. We enjoyed this diversion but never found out who he was. There were three lads in our cell at one time, one of whom had sung in pubs and he would take it turns with the mystery voice. They would stop suddenly, probably silenced by a warder.

In the early hours of one morning, we were woken by a prisoner screaming and throwing things about. The warders arrived and made even more noise. We could not see anything but as he was taken out of his cell it seemed he dived over the railings onto the wire netting suspended between the floors. There was no chance of sleeping through this disturbance and only a short time later, or so it seemed, it was time to get up. The usual method of being woken was for a warder to throw a metal bucket down the metal stairs from the top floor. It made enough noise to wake the dead and there was little chance of anyone not hearing the din that was made.

The first activity of each and every day was to 'slop-out' and have a wash and shave. Razors were kept outside the cells in case anyone got any ideas of using them for purposes other than shaving. One morning the staff examined clothing for lice. It appeared that some of the prisoners were infected and needed fumigating. If one person in a cell was found to have the problem, everyone in the cell had to be treated. I was one of ten who became involved and we were placed in the older part of the prison until we were pronounced clear. The cells in this section were lit by gas. At 10 o'clock each evening the gas, controlled from outside the cells, would be turned down so as to give only a glimmer of light. On one morning, all the men in our cell woke up with splitting headaches and feeling dreadful. The men in the adjacent cell suffered far worse and were carried out on stretchers. We never found out what happened to them. It would appear the night before the staff had turned the gas off completely and then merely turned it on again without relighting the lamps.

Christmas 1940 was spent in Shepton Mallet prison. Christmas Day was treated like a Sunday. There were no parades, only a church service in the chapel in the morning after which you were locked up for the rest of the day. Neither was the food any different. In the evening, the Salvation Army played Christmas carols at the prison gates. It was very emotional for me and I remembered my family and my own connections with the Salvation Army band. There was nothing tough about me that particular night.

The next morning it was back to normal, the staff yelling, '. . . On parade in five minutes, field service marching order. FSMO.' This was an impossibility as all equipment was laid out for inspection by the duty warders and we came out on parade in a complete shambles as they knew we would. We had had an easy time the day before and easy times in prison do not come often. Our punishment was being doubled around the yard for three solid hours without a break. As some of the men collapsed they were doused in cold water. I managed to keep going – but only just. At the time the prison yard was being dug up and was in a terrible state. Our best polished boots were in a shocking mess by the time we had finished and it took weeks to get them shining again.

You were only permitted to write home on prison notepaper which consisted of a single brown page with the prison rules and regulations on the reverse. Only a few ever wrote home and I was not one of them.

Prisoners shortly due for release were treated a little better. As a group we were taken around the prison and shown where men had been hanged, and how their bodies were collected in a barrow before being buried in a plot in the prison yard. We were introduced to an old warder who remembered the times when hangings took place in Shepton Mallet and shown the death cell where those sentenced to be hanged would spend their last weeks. The light would be left on at all times and two warders were on duty, day and night. Then there was the place where the actual execution was carried out. There was a big lever on the wall and when pulled a trapdoor opened onto a sixty-foot drop into the courtyard below. There were probably twenty graves each with a simple wooden cross. I am told that Shepton Mallet was the prison where they tried to hang the murderer, John Lee, without success. Apparently, three attempts were made, all failed and he was later released.

The day came for our release, a third of our sentence being remitted for good conduct. We were provided with four slices of bread – two with meat and two with marmalade in them – and given a pass to take us back to our unit. By way of a bonus we received a helping hand out of the gate from the big boot of a prison warder.

A little lad was waiting outside the prison and gave both Bill and me a packet of ten Woodbines each. His mother had sent him and he tried to help us carry our kit to the station. It was a kind gesture which we appreciated, all the more, after the harsh treatment on the inside.

We arrived back at the battalion depot, pending instructions to return to our main unit, and settled down to the usual infantry exercises. There had been a lot of recent arrivals and Bill and I helped with their training while awaiting our orders. We were amazed how they took notice. I thought they would consider we were really bad lads and that no one would want to listen to us. It was just the opposite.

The order to return to our battalion was received and every-thing was packed including bedding and blankets, ready for sending on ahead of us. On arrival, we went to collect our equipment and the blankets were missing. The sergeant major accused us of stealing them and put us on a charge. We were, of course, completely innocent and had been set up. In the meantime the battalion moved down to the south coast and there we were put on CO's orders. When the charge was heard, I was very worried that Bill would do something he would regret – he could be a hothead at times. The CO read out the charge and asked Bill if he would take his punishment or elect to face a court martial. Bill decided on the court martial. I was then asked the same question. My reply was that I would accept his award of punishment. I would swear the CO smiled. A court martial could have given a sentence of up to one year's detention against a maximum of one month by the CO.

Several weeks later, I was told I alone was being posted to join the Highland Division in Scotland. Bill and all the others in the company whom I had known for a long time were being sent to various other regiments. Just what happened to the officers I never found out. The mystery of the missing blankets also remains unsolved and I heard no more about my charge or Bill his court martial.

5

A Light at the End of the Tunnel

When I reported to the orderly room for the documents to take me to Scotland, I was informed that before going over the border I would be attached to the Hants Division for a time. This was a unit that dealt with all service affairs.

I travelled to Winchester where I was met at the station and taken to headquarters. The officer in charge shook hands, wished me well and said I would be based in Winchester and would work as a radio operator or a driver. In the battalion I had spent two years in peace time doing most things including Morse on lamp, buzzer and heliograph.

The unit consisted of men from different units but mainly from the Corps of Signals and everybody got on very well together which was most unusual. I spent hours riding over the hills on a motorcycle carrying messages. The unit held motorcycle rallies which were great fun. There was also a very good rugger team with two Cambridge blues and, after a test, I played prop-forward for them. I could not believe the change that had taken place in a matter of a week or so – from prison to playing rugby union with officers who sounded their aitches.

Despatch riders had to go occasionally into Southampton and Portsmouth in the evenings and were often caught up in bombing raids. On one night I was in the docks area of Southampton when the sirens had sounded, and I wondered whether to take cover since it was getting rather rough. I decided to press on and, although the streets were well lit with buildings ablaze, I did not see the hole my bike went down. When I picked my bike and myself up I found a dead cat was wedged between the tyre and mudguard. I like cats and this upset me more than the bombing.

During the winter of 1941 I was called into the orderly room by the officer in charge. He informed me the RAF were asking for volunteers for selection as fighter pilots. If I would like to sit the tests he would help me. I, of course, was very pleased to accept the opportunity.

The examinations consisted of a physical test and mathematics and English. My CO arranged for a tutor from Winchester College to give me lessons in maths in the evenings for a period of six weeks prior to the selection process. For the tests I travelled to an army camp in Oxford where there were twenty or so other volunteers taking part. The tests were undertaken at Magdalen College in Oxford. Two days were spent on physical examinations and a further two days for the mathematics and English. I wrote about *lease lend* – the arrangement with the USA for essential supplies of food and materials during the war. It had to be something topical. The examiner said he would pass my essay on to the government as he thought they might learn something from its contents. I passed the examinations but did not hear from the government. Five of the group passed and we went to an airfield outside Oxford for air experience. This consisted of being taken up in a Hurricane aeroplane for a period each day for three or four days. The actual time spent in the air depended on how well you took to being thrown about all over the sky. I thoroughly enjoyed every minute.

Before we broke up to go back to our units we were given the option of taking a four-jump parachute course at Ringway Airport in Manchester. It was desirable to take the course to become conversant with parachuting in case we had to bail out over Germany. We got a lot of advice such as 'You must be bloody crackers,' and 'It's bad enough going out when you have to, let alone as a hobby.' Nevertheless, we all decided to have a go.

We took up residence at Ringway Airport where we learned to roll, jump off balconies in a harness and out of a big hole which was supposed to represent an aircraft. The hole was about four feet in diameter and if you jumped too far forward you hit your nose – some chaps broke their noses. If you did not jump far enough forward you caught your parachute on your back and were thrown forward with the same result – a damaged nose. The correct procedure was to lift your legs up and thrust them down sharply, keeping your feet and knees together until you felt the tug of your 'chute opening.

Our first jump was from a balloon in Tatton Park. When I looked at it I felt queasy. My sister's boyfriend was in the RAF and in charge of the balloon from which I practised. We did not get on very well and he tried to wind me up, grinning from ear to ear – I must have made his day. The five of us for the jump, together with the instructor, got into the basket of the balloon. We ranged ourselves around the limited space. Some had only three inches on which to stand – I was one of them. Metal hand-holds were driven into the floor – two for each man. There were jokes about men being seen after landing with the metal holds still in their hands. I must admit I could see the possibility.

The instructor stood in the corner where a bar holding our straps was placed. Everyone was hooked up and checked by the instructor. I was to jump at no. 5. We went up and as we did we sang about someone landing on the tarmac like a load of strawberry jam. As we went higher the voices gradually died out until we reached 700 feet when there was not a sound but the wind. One by one we fell out of the balloon and successfully completed our first jump.

We then did three jumps from a Whitley aircraft to complete the course before returning to the camp at Oxford where we were congratulated on passing all the tests. We were also told that when more aircraft became available we would be transferred to the RAF. I returned to Winchester and received more congratulations from the officers and men of the Hants Division.

Christmas 1941 was very different to the previous one which was spent in Shepton Mallet. This time I had a choice how it was spent.

In February 1942, I was posted to Scotland, Western District where I did the same sort of job as in Winchester. My papers came through in May to join the 51st Highland Division who were then stationed at Farnborough, near Aldershot. I arrived at Aldershot station with all my gear including overcoat, small pack, big pack on my back, kitbag and two carrier bags when two military policemen came up to me: 'You soldier, do that top button up.' I had to take off all my gear to comply with their instruction. They let me dress before asking me for my rail warrant which was in an inside pocket. Again, I had to repeat the performance. Eventually they allowed me to go and I arrived at my unit which was the 154th Brigade Infantry.

I had left a unit where discipline was fairly lax and come to one which was just the opposite. It was a good thing that I had become accustomed to it in the Essex regiment. I was billeted in a hut that housed a platoon of Black Watch men. Clearly, they wondered what a sassenach was doing in their hut and it would seem I was not too popular, although no one said anything to me personally. On my first day, at teatime, I watched one platoon march off with men creeping behind knocking mess tins out of others' hands. I decided that should this happen to me, I would flatten the man behind me.

When it was our turn to parade I had my mess tins knocked out of my hands and so I whipped round and floored the man behind me. Lots of men dived on me and dragged me off. The sergeant went wild about a bloody sassenach daring to fight a Scotsman. I also put in my two pennyworth verbally and left them in no doubt what I thought of the Black Watch. After this episode, I got many queer looks but never any more bother marching to meals.

The day after my arrival, I went to the orderly room to check whether they knew of my waiting for my papers to join the RAF. They did and said I would be the first to know when they were received. With a big grin the orderly room sergeant said they were not likely to forget.

After a couple of weeks doing exercises and unarmed combat, the 51st started getting ready to move. Still there was no word from the RAF despite my hanging about the orderly room. We were informed we were to move on the last Sunday in May. All units gathered in a big hotel for a last drink together on the Saturday evening, and what an evening it was. There were Black Watch, Argylls, Seaforths, Gordons, Camerons and various other Highlanders. All were very partisan but they were kind enough to invite me along.

The next morning we left for Bristol and Avonmouth docks. After much hanging around we were ferried to a French ship named *SS Cuba*. It had a French captain and officers but the crew were English. We made ourselves at home on F deck, just above the waterline – a point we were to be thankful of during the voyage. Every man had a hammock which was very comfortable. I felt very queasy as I walked round the deck and was sick: this was before the ship even moved. A good laugh was had at my expense but I got my own back later when nearly every other person was sick except myself.

The *SS Cuba* sailed through the Irish Sea and up the River Clyde to join more ships gathering to form a convoy. Our ship lay at anchor between Gouroch and Greenoch and some of the lads on board lived nearby: it must have been hell for them and, inevitably, there were men who were absent on occasions.

We moved down the Clyde on 3 June and into the Atlantic. There were sixty-three ships, guarded by three very big ships and several cruisers and destroyers. Each company kept its men busy: a typical day would start at 9.00 a.m, with physical training on the aft well deck followed at 10 by Highland dancing – our company commander was a champion dancer and kept us at it – heel and toe and so on.

Later it would be weapon training with most of it done blindfolded and we became expert at changing barrels and reloading magazines. As the weather got warmer, we would organise games in the afternoons. Card schools were popular in the evenings with pontoon being the favourite. Five or six men would play and maybe a dozen would back 10/– or even £1 on their choice of player. A lot of money changed hands at these sessions.

Our washing would be hung out on a length of electric cable obtained from the stores. Our shirts, vests, pants and socks were fastened to the cable with one end fixed to a cleat inside the ship and the other passed through a porthole into the sea. I never knew of anyone losing his washing and it was always clean.

During the parade one morning the CO spoke to us over the tannoy system. There was a whole brigade on the ship and that was over 3,000 men. The brigadier said everything was going well, the men were in good spirits and it was intended that a series of boxing matches would be held in all the ships in the convoy. The winners of the heats would be taken to fight on the general's ship. The officer in charge of boxing on our ship then took over the talking and read out the names of the contestants for the different weights. He came to welter-weight and I was at the top of the list! I had not volunteered – someone had put my name down. I played hell, but they had me down on the list and there I was to stay. I was to fight a champion from the Argylls whom I had seen in action and considered a very good boxer. It was not that I was frightened – I was not a bad fighter myself, but not with gloves. I was a street fighter.

Before the fight there were some sly smiles amongst the men I had jumped on the first day. The aft deck was packed for the contest with everybody not on duty attending. Rows of officers were seated at the front. When it came to my turn, a very big cheer went up for my opponent as he stepped into the ring. I climbed in and a few men cheered from my platoon. It was not until I was seated in my corner that I made up my mind how to avoid getting a good hiding. In army boxing you come out of your corner, touch gloves and commence boxing. Boxing booths at fairgrounds do not cater for such niceties – you just come out fighting straightaway. That was the answer to the problem.

We were called to the middle of the ring and warned, no holding, no hitting low, may the best man win and all that stuff and then returned to our corners. The bell went and we both came out, and went to touch gloves. Instead I hit good and hard and down he went – completely out. Everybody was yelling and shouting and some of the officers invaded the ring protesting to the referee. I explained to the referee my previous experience at fairgrounds and he assured the officers that this was correct. They, eventually, accepted his decision. My name had been put down so that I would get a hiding and I had turned the tables on them. In fact I had been boxing in the army for six years. Meanwhile my opponent had come round and insisted the fight was resumed. After much debate it was decided it would. I smiled and said, 'Why not?'. I let the fight go on for a couple of rounds, giving him a reminder now and again that I was in charge. At the start of the third round he came at me like a windmill and I had to weather the storm and await my chance. He got me in a corner with me taking blows on hands and arms. I watched his feet through my gloves and he moved back a couple of paces when I flew at him: this time I downed him good and proper – and legally. From then on it was Fred Memmott, the Yorkshire Scrapper. There's nowt so funny as folk!

The ship arrived in Freetown, Sierra Leone, and anchored in the bay with the rest of the convoy. The natives came out in their bum boats and tried to sell fruit, eggs, wicker baskets and handbags made of crocodile leather. Goods would be sent up in a basket attached to a rope and if you wanted to buy the item money would be sent back down. Young lads would dive for coins, preferably silver, in the sea. Our lads would wrap halfpennies in silver paper and the boys would go wild when they found out. It was a good job there was a distance between us.

The evenings were humid and the mosquitoes came out in their millions. We were given some ointment to put on our hands and faces but it only attracted them to a greater extent. The best place was down below for a game of cards. As we went further south the sea went into massive rollers: the ship would go down on one roller and up on the next with spray flying all over. It was very exciting.

One night we were in our hammocks when the alarm bell sounded. Everyone got up and made a dash for the stairs that went up to the next deck, only to run into the men of the deck below, and so on. Men from four decks were trying to get to C deck where the lifeboats were stationed. It was jam packed and if it had been the real thing I cannot see how we would have survived.

The sun was just rising when the convoy approached Capetown. Table Mountain stood there in all its glory and you could see the cable cars going up to Kloof Neck. It was a sight well worth seeing and one I will never forget. There were crowds of people cheering us as we docked. We were allowed ashore in the afternoon and men were being picked up by civilians and taken to their homes. In our party there were three of us and we were invited to join a middle-aged lady and her two daughters in a lovely black car. We were made very welcome and driven to a big house that had gilded gates and marble pillars on the walls. The three of us were taken to the bathroom together. It had a sunken bath, more like a swimming pool with plenty of room for all three. When we came out of the bath a black woman wrapped us in hot towels and was not perturbed in the slightest that we were starkers.

Then it was into the drawing room where we were asked many questions about England and how things were going there. Were people worried about the war, they asked. Not at all, we replied, we would win. About 7 p.m. dinner was served – we were starving. The dining room had wooden doors in one wall which were open and two black women served the dishes from the kitchen to the one who placed them on the table. It was an excellent meal and all the family was good company. The young girls played the piano for us and we were shown photographs of South Africa. We left with a good impression of life in South Africa. After exchanging addresses and promising to write, the lady drove us back to the ship as we had to be back by midnight.

I was on duty the next day, but the following day I went out on my own and met a lady who whisked me off to a big house in the hills. The lady's son, Jerry, was an officer in the South African army and was on leave from fighting in Abyssinia. In peacetime he had played rugger for the Springboks and so we had plenty to talk about. I had a pleasant day and they made me very welcome. Jerry ran me back to the docks and Mrs Brandt packed me up with cakes and cigarettes.

On the last day in Capetown, we were warned that the boat would be sailing at 6 a.m. the following morning and there would be trouble should we not return in time. The three of us who first went ashore together went into a bar for a few beers and met a sergeant in the South African army: he suggested he should take us to District 6 to the *shabeens* where coloured men drank in their hundreds. It sounded interesting and off we went.

As we went down one street lined with shops and other buildings, two cars squealed to a stop outside a big dance hall. About half a dozen men got out and ran up the stairs, returning minutes later dragging two men who were protesting loudly. They were thumped and then bundled into the cars. On asking around, we were told the men in the cars were the local police. All were black as was everybody who lived in District 6. It was not unlike what we had seen in the gangster films of the American prohibition.

We went through District 6 and came to a tented area. There were two massive tents, like circus tents, joined together. We went in and the place was packed with black people drinking. There were masses of trestle tables with wooden forms at which people were seated. Hurricane lamps lit the area and threw shadows giving a kaleidoscope of light and dark over the place. We had a very interesting evening propping up one of the long bars that went around the sides of the tents. The stewards provided us with an escort back to the ship where we arrived at about 2.30 a.m. After only a few hours sleep we sailed on our way but no one among the lower ranks knew where we were heading.

6

Into Egypt

We thought we could be heading for either India or Egypt. After a couple of days sailing we had a 'free-from-infection' inspection and having been passed in order we carried on with our usual exercises – weapon training, map reading, sport and interior economy. The latter consisted of keeping yourself and your kit in good order.

The convoy passed through the Indian Ocean heading north and both the sunrises and sunsets were something not to be missed: *glorious* is an inadequate word to describe the sight each time. Every morning lots of flying fish would be lying on deck. We spent a lot of time watching them jumping and gliding for maybe a hundred yards or so through the air.

After a few days sailing the convoy split into two with one part heading for India and ourselves for Egypt. Several days later we arrived at the port of Aden for refuelling which was done by hand. Two gangways were let down to the dock and a continual line of men went up one, carrying coal or wood, and down the other, having dropped their load. This went on all day and was a regular thing at various ports. While this was taking place we were allowed ashore. First, we went to the NAAFI club where you could have a swim and a meal. The pool had a shark net stretched across its mouth and if a shark managed to get through an alarm bell would ring. We had been in the water only a few minutes when the alarm went off and I have never seen people move so quickly – myself included. One minute must have seen the pool completely empty. The meal afterwards was not as exciting as the swimming.

When we returned to the ship in the evening the refuelling was complete and the next morning we were off into the Red Sea. It was August and extremely hot. We were encouraged to get a tan before we arrived at our destination to avoid later problems of burnt arms and backs which would interfere with our fitness as soldiers.

We docked at the port of Tewfick at the bottom end of the Suez Canal a few days later and were taken off the ship in lighters and then marched to the railway line where we waited for the train to arrive. There were about 3,000 men waiting and the train arrived after about an hour. We boarded and travelled alongside the canal, passing through several villages and fields growing crops. Almost all had an animal on a sort of a yoke going round and round and drawing water from a well. A lad sat on the yoke with the animal. It must have been monotonous. Much further on we started to pass what, I believe, were German prisoner of war camps. The men inside the compounds made rude gestures accompanied by much shouting. Our lads shouted back, 'You have had it now, we have come to settle your hash'.

Darkness came and most men dozed off. It was around 2 or 3 a.m. when the train came to a halt and we alighted, waiting nearby for daylight to come. When it did we found we were close to an enormous camp of tents and wooden buildings. We were allocated accommodation and one of the first things I did was to visit the orderly room and enquire how I stood about my transfer to the Royal Air Force. I was informed that, owing to our moving to the Middle East Command, it would not be possible for me to be sent back to England. To say I was upset was to put it mildly. I was fuming and requested a transfer to the Airborne there and then. What else could I do but get drunk – which I did. I found out later that the letter from RAF had arrived at Brigade HQ about a week before we left Avonmouth but had been put aside since they did not want to lose anyone: they were at full strength and determined to stay that way. I was devastated.

After a couple of night marches under the stars and various lectures on finding our way about the desert, the 51st prepared to move 'up the blue'. This meant move into the desert. We went up the main road to Alexandria and turned off into the desert at Klm 130. It was a very poor track which had been heavily used by vehicles. An hour or so later we passed a big compound enclosed by fencing and, to our surprise, the men who had jumped ship at Gouroch were there waiting for us to arrive. They had been caught and brought out on the *Queen Mary*, which because of its faster speed had arrived before us. They joined our group.

As we got nearer the front line we could hear guns muttering in the distance. We pulled into a *wadi* and settled ourselves there. Some men were sent on to the Aussie line, which was near the front, to collect intelligence and report back. After a couple of weeks we moved up and took over our share of the front line that consisted of mine boxes. These were staggered alternately from the coast to the Quattara Depression. The 51st took over three boxes.

We were allowed four days' leave in Cairo. When my turn came we were taken across the desert to join a train which had stopped in the middle of nowhere and was joined by troops from Australia, New Zealand and South Africa. It was a very riotous four days and something to remember.

There was a fair amount of vegetation at one of the places where we camped and someone spotted a little creature that seemed very vicious. It hissed and blew itself up to nearly twice its size. After studying it carefully. I picked it up between thumb and forefinger. Nothing happened, it stopped hissing and re-duced in size. I took a fancy to it and put it on my shoulder where it appeared to be quite content. There were flies around and it seemed very happy just catching and eating them. It had a very long tongue that was sticky on the end and the flies had no chance at all. Its bulbous eyes moved independently of each other. I later found out it was a chameleon. He disappeared when I put him down to have a cup of tea and it took ages to find him again. The way he changed colour to match the background was fascinating. I put a piece of white tape on his tail that helped me to keep track of him for a while but I lost him during the fighting at El Alamein.

Someone got the idea that it would be a good thing for us to march up in small numbers to the coast for a swim and a clean up. It was about fifteen miles away and by the time you got back to your mine box you were just as dirty and sweaty as you ever had been. The idea was scrapped.

The 51st was moved further north just below the coast road and this was to be our position for mounting an attack. One day we went to visit a dressing station beyond Alamein where we picked up our water. Tanks were lined up, just off the road, some made up to look like trucks and some as water wagons. Jerry spotter planes would think that they were as they were meant to look – soft transport. I understood that trucks going south were made to look like tanks. If the Germans believed the deception, their armour would be down south and we would attack from the north. On 23 October 1942, at 9 p.m., one gun was fired and that let loose the biggest artillery barrage I ever heard. It was awful and when our guns opened up so did the Germans, and we were in the middle. It seemed we were getting it from both sides. When dawn broke the next morning it was something I did not expect to see and there must have been many others who felt the same. The gory details of the fighting, wounding and dying I will leave to others to relate. I just happened to be there and had to make the best of it, as did many other men.

We had been told before the attack that if we advanced seven miles we would be through, but after travelling seven-and-a-half miles we had only just come up to the main defence line. Stuka aircraft bombed us without mercy and many men became buried when the soft sand of the trenches gave way. After that we were ordered that no trench in that area would be more than two feet deep which was just enough to get you below ground level. From then on it was a really hard slog, advancing when and how you could. There was much sniping by the enemy and sometimes it was hard to judge where they were. To me, the end of the Battle of Alamein was as surprising and spectacular as the beginning. It was night and it had gone unusually quiet. We were resting in a trench and attempting to get some sleep when the sky was filled with tracer shells in the form of Vs for victory. It was a marvellous feeling and like getting permission to live a little longer. The Germans and the Italians had flown, with some of our men and the New Zealanders hard on their heels.

We then moved a few miles to Fuka near the coast. This area was hilly and had a fair amount of vegetation. Hyenas lived in the hills and were a real pain at night with their so-called laughing. For a few days it was very pleasant but I began to get restless and wanted to do something. A day or so later I was asked by the officer in charge if I would like a trip on my own to find an advance party of the 51st who were in the Tobruk area. I jumped at the opportunity and was provided with a motorcycle and two days' rations. My first stop was near the Egyptian border with Libya at a place called Bug-Bug. The NAAFI had set up a big tent there and I got a cup of tea. Petrol stations had been positioned along the road that consisted of piled up four-gallon petrol cans where you helped yourself after speaking to the man in charge. I went along Sollum Pass and up into Libya through Derna and it was getting dark by the time I approached Tobruk, having covered well over 300 miles, maybe nearer 400, and filled up with petrol twice. Everyone who was travelling had pulled up for the night and I put my bike into a ditch, had a sandwich and kipped down until it was light again. Life was very simple in those days.

Tanks were moving up the coast on low loaders when I woke up the next morning and after a wash, shave and a tin of bully beef, I set off for Tobruk. When I got there it was nothing as I imagined it would be. I started asking around if anyone had seen Scotsmen wearing hats like mine. Much time was spent asking individuals around Tobruk for information and I was getting desperate when someone suggested they might be up around Gazala. It was worth a try and I went off in that direction and came to a point where a new road was being built by the Italians. I asked around and one Italian replied, 'Ah, men with funny hats like yours. Yes, I see some up that new road.' I continued on my way and reached El Adem where there was an airfield containing several tents. Sure enough, they were the men for whom I had been searching. I saw an officer and delivered a message in a thick packet. He told me the 51st had moved up to Fort Cappuzo near the Egyptian border. I looked at his map and decided I would make my way back along the Trigh-Capuzzo track that was a short cut but very wild country with big herds of wild camels. After replenishing my food supplies I said cheerio and went on my way.

Passing the airfield at El Adem I saw many burnt-out planes belonging to the Germans. A small transit camp had been set up there and I decided to see if it was possible to get a meal and stop overnight. I was made most welcome, was given a meal and a rope bed. The next morning I was up early, had some breakfast and was on my way with about 200 odd miles to go. The track I was taking became gradually more rutted the further I went, but I made good time. I must have gone about half-way when I saw hundreds of camels – small, medium and large. They all seemed to be looking at me and my bike. The nearer I got, the less brave I became. I could not blast my way through them as the ground was too bumpy and 5 mph was about the limit you could travel safely. They were all around me and bumping me with their great legs. When the track started to get more even, I thought about opening the throttle but remembered that camels are capable of moving very fast and decided to be cautious. I was getting low on fuel when I spotted a convoy of trucks coming towards me with my train of camels. The convoy and I met head on. The driver of the lead truck said I should take my bike along the convoy and continue on my way – the camels would then follow them in the opposite direction. I was pleased they did so and I was able to continue my return journey.

It was getting dark by the time I returned and reported to our orderly room. The officer in charge congratulated me and said that if I carried on like this I would do well. I smiled and replied, 'Don't forget my transfer, sir. Need I say more?

The following day the whole division moved by road to where I had delivered the package. We travelled through the western desert with 80 to 100 yards between vehicles so that if a bomb hit one truck, damage would be limited. There was nowhere to hide in the desert. The division formed up in many long lines and well dispersed. Each lead truck had a light mounted high above the cab that all in that line could see and the centre truck had three different coloured lights for travelling in the dark. It worked very well – like a convoy at sea. We cut across the desert from El Adam to a place well south of Benghazi and made good time travelling all day and all night with only a few stops for attention to mother nature. It was an order that everybody who wanted to wee had to climb onto a truck and do so into the radiator since water was scarce. No truck ever broke down through lack of water.

We joined the coast road again which we had left behind at Tobruk and as we passed through Agedabia, which was only a small place, we saw little Union Jacks were in the windows.

How nice, we thought. Our driver who had been through here previously said, 'Don't get too excited, when Jerry comes through here they put little swastikas in their windows.' Some time later we turned off the road and went to the sand hills by the sea: we had arrived. Guns began to rumble just to prove the point. We moved from there, on foot, to take over from the men who had chased Jerry all this way and done a good job. It took some time to settle down, finding out where the defences were situated and in what strength.

Christmas came and we heard rumours that each man would be given two cans of beer. We thought Montgomery must be going soft in the head. Up to now he had only allowed ammunition, petrol, bully beef and hard tack. He must want something from us, we thought. Christmas Day was quiet and we assembled for lunch, each of us receiving two bottles of beer. An officer gave a short speech, then in came the cooks carrying big dixies and flanked by two pipers who gave a great rendering of *Highland Laddie*. The cooks then dished out the dinner with a big ladleful for each man. A tremendous roar went up from the men. No one had seen bully stew piped in before but we saw the amusing side and the beer went down well.

Jerry left us alone. Eventually, we went in with an attack but it took three days to clear the mines and the men got a rollicking for letting Jerry get away. This must not happen again was the order. That we had sent him flying did not seem to matter. Nufilia was an old-fashioned Arab walled city, very big with many towers. None of us was allowed to enter but we had a good view from the hills. It was a mysterious looking place. A young Arab was out on the hills with a lovely white stallion and he allowed one of our chaps to ride it for a short while.

Before we went into the desert to go up to Misurata we had passed some airfields and over the coast road there was an enormous wooden arch that had been erected by the Italians.

Our men nicknamed it Marble Arch. There must have been thousands of signatures either written on it or cut into its surface and it looked so out of place in that area. Misurata was another town with palm trees at the sides of the roads. We carried on for another twenty miles or so before coming under machine gun fire. In front of us was a deep chasm that cut right across our path and the bridge crossing had been destroyed.

It does not take many men to use a couple of machine guns and a couple of mortars to halt whoever is chasing them: the pursuers have to halt, sort out what they are up against and then decide how best to deal with the threat. It takes time and gives the main body of the retreating troops time to escape. The chasm took a while to cross. A steep track went down on both sides which was the old way from before the bridge had been built. Big Scammel trucks were positioned at the top of both tracks: one to aid trucks going down and the other to pull them up. It worked fine but it took three days to cover a couple of miles.

The countryside grew more attractive as we approached Tripoli. We were also starving as rations had not caught up with us. For breakfast one morning we were given one packet of hard tack biscuits and a tin of sardines to share among three men. We were assured we would be given extra rations as soon as they arrived. On the outskirts of Tripoli we were ordered to halt and sat by the roadside wondering why when a truck containing military police went by. We all laughed as they were likely to be the first British troops in Tripoli. Just imagine – Tripoli taken by MPs! Later, an armoured column came by, carrying the 11th Hussars: they were given the honour of taking Tripoli.

7

Libya and Tunisia

All units and divisions gathered around Tripoli and we were told there was to be a big victory parade. Our brigade was detailed to guard the route both on the ground and from the tops of the buildings. My unit was to be stationed on the rooftops opposite a big fort with two stone columns with the figures of Romulus and Remus on top. It was quite an imposing place.

The day arrived and we went into Tripoli, debussing in the centre of the city where there was plenty of space. We felt very proud marching to the fort with the pipers on show. Up onto the roofs we went with orders to show anyone we met up there the shortest way down, but not by way of the front of the building. The dignitaries' platform, where they would take the salute, was directly opposite and our orders were to guard them in no mistaken fashion. We were all marksmen and ready for any eventuality.

The parade commenced with tanks that were followed by armoured cars, various artillery and an assortment of trucks. All were polished and in pristine condition. The parade seemed to go on and on. I did not know we had so many tanks and so much artillery. Then we spotted some of our vehicles coming round for a second time and realised what was happening. Apparently, the Germans had pulled the same stunt when they arrived in Tripoli at the time of the introduction of the Afrika Korps: they had started the campaign with under a hundred tanks – the British thought they had over two hundred. We had an excellent view of the parade from our position on the roofs and thoroughly enjoyed the day. The parade finished with lots of hip, hip, hoorays for the top brass.

Our unit returned to camp and the next day we were given a day's leave. We were dropped in the centre of the city and a pal and I did some shopping. Shops and stalls had opened again in spite of the fact that Jerry planes poked their noses in occasionally. That afternoon, in a big open square, some New Zealanders started a tossing ring. Men who wished to play and bet on the game formed a big square and a couple of dozen New Zealanders ran the game: two supervising the tossing of the coins and the rest collecting the money, paying out and making sure everyone behaved properly. The money was collected in sandbags and there were hundreds playing the game. I managed to win a fair amount.

Near where we were playing was the end of a queue which must have stretched almost half a mile and was about nine men deep. We were told it was for a local brothel and there were six well-worn Italian women who were really trying to do their best for the troops. Next please, next please, next . . . We could not keep count.

In the evening we were drinking in a cafe with some South Africans and New Zealanders when a chap came in who had been beaten up and had his money stolen. Everyone was sorry for him and helped to patch him up. A collection was taken for him in a big hat and it was stuffed with money. He probably finished with more than he had before he was mugged and also more than any of us.

On the following day we prepared to move. As we rolled out of the plantation where we had been staying we wondered where and when we would catch up with Jerry again. The countryside we travelled through was pleasant – palm trees, green grass and old farms with animals and crops. We went through a place called Ben Gardane and continued going west.

It was interesting to see how the 8th Army managed to keep vehicles on the move. A truck would be blown up by a mine when taking a short cut, and before the dust had settled, men would be there removing anything of value. Even engines were removed very quickly. Cannibalisation was the order of the day and a first class expertise was developed.

We stopped near a town named Medenine with mountainous country in the distance and moved on foot to the west of the town where we waited until nightfall. Officers informed us that the brigade would take up positions that were in full view of the enemy and so no noise whatsoever was to be made. The mountain we were in the lee of was very high with a white hut on the top. I should imagine it was a good lookout place. We were stopped and told that there would be no movement during daylight and no more than three or four men would be in any one place together. The following day was quiet until the evening when Jerry let into us with his 88s and many air bursts. At times like these we would crouch three men in a dog-leg trench with one man at each end and one man in the middle. The idea was to crouch in a corner with your legs up and arms wrapped round them and your tin hat on, trying to cover up. It surprised me how we got away with it so often. Turns were taken to be the middle man because he could be hit from both sides. Ammunition had to be collected from time to time and this involved three men carrying two boxes with 1,000 rounds in each box. You could guarantee if you were above ground Jerry would start firing. This sort of thing went on for several weeks. The Germans had good defensive positions and we could not go forward willy-nilly.

As full moon neared we expected trouble from the enemy and, sure enough, it came. We were heavily shelled and lost a fair number of our men as a result. Then Jerry attacked with his Tiger tanks between our brigade and the division to our left. It was a bit rough – to say the least. His tanks passed us and went hell for leather for the airfield at Medenine. Unfortunately for him, the New Zealanders had seized the airfield with their Medium guns – 4.5 and 5.5s. These guns were a blessing to the 8th Army. As the Tigers attacked the airfield, the New Zealanders opened fire over open sights and that set the cat among the pigeons. The Tiger tanks could not take it and were knocked out. They withdrew.

We had been cut off during the attack on the airfield, but now we launched a counter-attack and made a little headway. After two or three days of fighting it went quiet and it was a case of watching each other's movements. Then the 8th Army made their preparations for an attack.

The Guards Brigade made a feint south of the line next to us and 50th Division attacked to the north but these came to nothing. We, the 51st, were pulled out of our positions and moved north to relieve 50th Division. As we met the men of 50 Division coming back we saw they were in a bad way. The Germans were extremely careful with us and kept quiet for a good while.

We, the 154th Brigade, were pulled out for a break and got into a *wadi* that Jerry must have overlooked. It was quiet and we played cards in the open without worry. We had a couple of pleasant days, then one evening we were playing solo and suddenly a shower of shells burst around us. 'That's it,' we yelled. 'Jerry has handed over the guns to the Italians. He's ready for off.' To explain: the Germans only fired when they knew someone was there but when the Italians got hold of the guns they would fire at anything and everything. We therefore knew the Germans had handed over the guns and were ready for moving on, using the Italians as pawns. The Italians then bore the brunt of our attack and we moved forward very quickly.

We hardly noticed the village of Mareth as we went through – a very small place. One coastal town after another fell to our forces. We met up with the French Foreign Legion at one place. They had marched up from Lake Chad in the south and looked very fit. The Germans again made a stand at a place called Wadi Akarit and we were attacked for the first time by the 'moaning minnies' – a multiple mortar. I thought it sounded like a trumpeting elephant, but others had different ideas how it sounded. As the 'melody' finished mortar bombs splattered around you. We did not think much to them.

About 20,000 Italians had gathered together and marched through the lines to give themselves up. The Germans opened up on them with everything they had. It was absolute chaos. Trying to dodge German guns, the Italians ran into minefields and set off mines. Gradually, very gradually, things quietened down and the clearing up of the battlefield began. Each unit sent out its men to check the dead and collect their identity tags. Not a pleasant job and one that was shared. Dead men's few belongings were placed in sandbags and labelled. When you looked at the heap of sandbags, representing those you had known, you felt very small and if anyone spoke to you then it was difficult to reply.

After this the 51st gathered a few miles further on for a rest and sorting out. Some evenings a man on a wireless set in the Signals section would pick up the Forces network. It was more than likely Vera Lynn would come on and, if she did, she would be shut off immediately. I have seen her and her songs upset more men than the Germans ever did. In the desert she was known as Hitler's secret weapon.

We had a parade and a general inspected the men. He stopped in front of some of my mates. One was from Manchester, one from Newcastle and one from Leeds and they all looked very smart. He said, 'My, you can always tell a Highlander can't you!' I rest my case.

The division carried on moving west and the countryside was changing to olive groves and had that lovely smell associated with olive oil. In every village there was a swimming pool where olives were crushed and made into oil. I met one old boy who rode a camel and claimed to be a hundred years old. He said it was due to using olive oil. I have used it on every opportunity since. I met up with the old boy again a few days later in a village called El Djem, which was not far from Sousse. He collected old clothing, jerseys and shirts of any colour and the women would make rugs out of the materials. The finished article was very good.

I was called into the office in connection with my transfer to the Airborne Division. The campaign in Africa was almost over with the German Afrika Korps squashed between the 8th Army and the 1st Army which had landed in Morocco. It was just a case of mopping up and the Airborne was stationed reasonably close. My hopes were raised but, again, they came to nothing.

30 Corps was sending men back to Cairo to escort and guard officers who were taking part in the planning for the invasion of Sicily. I was asked to take a party and we were expected to stay about six weeks. Living for the day, I jumped at the chance. We set a target of 250 miles per day, resting for the night and then setting off again the first thing next morning. The total journey was 2,500 miles. We had almost reached Tripoli when we had trouble with our trucks but the mechanics worked hard and got them working again. When we reached the village of Agedabia we decided to keep to the coast road into Benghazi as going across the desert to Tobruk was thought to be too much for our old trucks. The column limped into Benghazi and was fortunate to run into the Mechanical Engineers who repaired our trucks. We continued to Alexandria by way of Alamein where we stopped and held a short service of thanksgiving for those who had died in the removal of the Afrika Korps.

We passed units of engineers who were clearing the desert of knocked-out units – wagons, tanks, etc. They were using big Scammel trucks and were towing eight or ten units at a time. We gave them a cheer.

Only three days behind schedule, we arrived in Alexandria and settled down for the night in the Mohammed Ali barracks on the seafront. We could not wait to get into the showers and clean ourselves up. Full of joys we did so, running around with nothing on. We were then told there were Gurkha troops also taking showers and their religion did not allow the removal of their shorts. So we put ours back on to be friendly which they appreciated with big smiles.

The next day saw our arrival in Cairo. Our convoy was escorted to the Kasrenil barracks where we stayed for several weeks. The officer I was detailed to escort was a 30 Corps man and I saw a lot of him. At night we would keep close watch on the building and also on anyone lurking around, however innocent they appeared. After the first few nights, strangers were noticeable by their absence. They had got the message – admittedly we had been a bit rough.

Life in Cairo had its pleasant moments. My friends and I regularly went to Groppi's for lunch and there were some quite nice bars where you could have a good drink. The attraction at Groppi's was the belly dancers, very eastern and good looking. They danced around while you ate, wiggled their bottoms and gyrated their tummies. They could have fed us bully stew and we would not have noticed the difference. We enjoyed the navel exercise.

The barracks were also first class. Clean clothes every day: you left them outside the door at night and they would be returned in the morning duly cleaned. In Cairo we did not do any walking but took a *gharri* everywhere. It was a great time but we knew it could not go on forever and six weeks saw the work completed. We were paraded, thanked for a good job and instructed how we would return to our units. Our return to 30 Corps was by truck and we were told we need not rush.

We took the opportunity to see the Pyramids and the Sphinx, knowing we were unlikely to see them again.

As our truck passed the NAFFI at Bug-Bug we decided to have a char and wad for old time's sake and then moved out of Egypt into Libya as we moved up through Sollum Pass. We were grinding our way up the pass when we saw the New Zealanders coming towards us. They had on the front truck a big white bust of Mussolini – the Italian dictator. With much cheering we went our separate ways.

Miles on, having passed through Derna and Tobruk and travelling towards Barce Pass, we settled down for a meal and were suddenly surrounded by millions of locusts. Not able to fly, only walk, the whole earth seemed to be heaving up and down with their presence. We gave up and went on to the salt flats at Benghazi.

Eventually we arrived back at our unit near Sousse. An officer from 30 Corps who had been with us on the Cairo trip told me that I had been transferred to 30 Corps and I would be driving and escorting him. Again I enquired about my transfer to Airborne and was told it would be considered when Sicily had been taken.

The 8th Army had settled into their marshalling area and life was quiet pending instructions for the invasion of Sicily. I visited most of the units at different times taking an officer here and there. Visiting the airfields at Kairouan was most interesting and I got to know some Americans very well. I was at one airfield chatting to some Yanks and I wanted some water. There was a big tank about 30 feet high stuck on the sand and I was told to fill my mug from it. I found the tap and turned it on: the contents were rusty. I returned and told them and they burst out laughing. The liquid in the tank was orangeade. The Yanks seemed to have everything: plenty of money, goods and, now, orangeade. Their government certainly looked after them. To top it, I was asked if I could get the weekend off to fly home. It was common practice to leave in a plane on a Friday night, arrive in England on Saturday morning, landing near Bury St Edmunds, have a night out in London and travel back to Kairouan on the Sunday, ready for work on Monday morning. I was not able to accept their offer.

There was plenty of opportunity for bathing in the sea, although we gradually grew tired of doing so. I was fortunate to have a day shopping in Tunis and a good meal. Casbahs in all Middle Eastern cities were always out of bounds so you could not get to know the natives. When I got back to my unit I learned that there had been a little excitement – the ammunition dump belonging to the Airborne had gone up.

8

The Overrunning of Sicily

There did not appear to be any real determination by the Germans or the Italians to prevent us from invading the island of Sicily. Infantry divisions, both British and American, made good headway once they had landed.

The airborne operation could have been better organised, but nevertheless, the invasion got under way and into the countryside. During this operation I was not involved in any fighting. I was now with 30 Corps HQ and spent my time visiting our own divisions, the 50th, and the 51st Infantry and the 7th Armoured. I also accompanied my officer to see how the Americans were managing: someone had to keep tabs on them!

When the 51st Highland Division were fighting on the slopes of Mount Etna it was impossible to dig slit trenches as the terrain was so rocky and slaty. Instead they built cairns in which they crouched and used them as gun pits.

It was so different being in Sicily. I had my first meal on a farm and it was really good. This was something not possible in North Africa. The Indian soldiers used mule trains to transport goods over the mountains. I met them occasionally and had a curry with them: if you could not eat three chapattis stuffed with hot curry you were not a welcome visitor. I had eaten with them in the desert and was made very welcome.

As 30 Corps moved up the eastern side of Sicily, support was given by Canadian tanks. The roads on some of the mountains were a bit dodgy and I have seen tanks topple over and go down into the valley, with one of the commanders getting chopped in half. One night I was in a truck with some men going over a mountain and we had to stop to let through an armoured column. We decided to have a meal. From the rations we had we soon got a hot meal going and the lovely smell of cooking filled the air. We gathered round the fire, ready to start the meal, and a young man in the black robes of a priest, wearing the usual black hat, approached us. He told us he was starving and had not eaten for days – could we help him. We thought, here was another scrounger, but he then did something which was unbelievable. He had his wife with him and offered her as payment for the meal. They were really hungry but there was no way we could accept his offer. She was a shy young girl and after the meal we took them both to the next town to be among their own folk.

We moved to the centre of Sicily and met up with the Americans. It was interesting watching them take one town that was on the top of a big hill. They sat on the top of the next hill, blasted away with their artillery for two days and then, when there was nothing left of the town higher than two feet, they moved in. Very few men were lost and the Americans always had plenty of ammunition.

Making our way to the north of Sicily, we turned right to get to Messina, which is a port near the toe of the Italy. At that point a two-mile stretch of water separates Sicily and Italy. The 8th Army had made good progress. 30 Corps pulled up in the hills behind Messina and I wondered why but was told to wait and see.

Some of our troops were stationed near to Catania where there was an airfield. It was a big, pleasant city, and on the route of a daily run to keep HQ in touch which we took in turns. On one of my trips, I turned on to the east coast road that led all the way to Catania and was flagged down by a young woman. She asked if I could help her get to Catania as there was no transport due to the fighting. We had been told not to upset the civilians if possible but it depended how you interpreted this order. I decided to pick her up. She had lots of grapes in a basket and fed me with them throughout the journey. At the Town Hall in Catania I dropped her off and she took me in to see her father. He was the mayor and could not thank me enough. His daughter had been visiting an aunt in Messina and could not get home. I saw the mayor leading a parade in the town some time later. The daughter was also there with her husband and two little girls. They all gave me a wave, and so did the father.

On another day I went down to the docks in Messina and met up with some of the Americans I had known on the Kairouan airfields. I went on board their ship and got absolutely blotto. I was having a couple of days' leave and was OK to stay on board and have some good food and drink.

Back at my unit, on top of the hills, I would often look over to Italy and watch our medium guns as they shelled targets in Italy. I was given orders to take my jeep to pick up my officer one evening at about 9 p.m. The Americans were invading Italy that evening and my officer was to accompany them and make out a report. There were thousands of Americans with masses of tanks, guns and trucks. What a noise they made. It seemed all confusion and you wondered if it would ever sort itself out. However, the next day with the Americans advancing on all fronts we returned to Sicily and our own unit.

Going south one day, along the east coast road, I went into a little village to see if I could get a meal, but was directed inland to another village. Here I saw a large shed that had 'Motor Engineering' on the side. Across the front in large letters was the name, FREDERICO MEMMOTTI. After this I was known as Frederico. The chap even looked similar to me, was about my height and, like me, had dark wavy hair. He gave me a meal on the house and we had a good chat. All the Sicilians I spoke to I seemed to get on with. The authorities had warned about them being jealous over their women. Most of us watched our step in this respect but, unfortunately, some did not.

I was travelling through a village one day when I came across a crowd of civilians gathered around some soldiers. Pulling over, I went to see what was going on. Two men were circling each other, the civilian with a hammer and the soldier with an axe in his hand. There were a few soldiers in the crowd and so I advised one to put an end to this sort of behaviour. These soldiers were engineers and were stationed in the village. They said the argument had been building up for some time and they would sort it out in their way. So I continued on my way. I often wonder how it all ended.

The roads over the mountains were at times little more than tracks. A mate and I were travelling over one and we were in a bit of a hurry. I was putting my foot down hard and as we neared the top of the mountain going round the bend we ran out of road. The hill went down steeply and so did our jeep. I braked very hard and, gradually, we pulled up at a crazy angle. We scarcely dared move for a time but my mate crept out over the back and went to fetch a Scammel truck we had passed a few minutes previously. There was a Scammel on the top of every hill for the purpose of helping clowns like me, who pushed it at times. After what seemed an age, I heard the truck come round the hill and pull up. One of the men got out, took the hook in his hand, pulled the cable down to where I sat and fastened the hook underneath our vehicle. He told me not to get upset, it happened often and that they had not lost anybody yet. With a wave to his mate our jeep was pulled slowly back up the hill. After thanks all round we continued our journey – at a much steadier pace. I do not know what the 8th Army would have done without the help of the Scammel.

A few days later our unit had orders to move to a village high on the hills, looking down on the sea. Wending our way up the steep road to the village, the view was terrific. We were so high, the sea was very blue and the ships passing looked like toys. Our billet was a big hotel in a village with the name of Taormina – a lovely place with old-fashioned cobbled streets which only mules could climb. This was our home for a few weeks before returning to England. It was just like being on holiday: much laughter and drinking in the bars and a good time was had by everyone. All things, good, bad and indifferent come to an end and this was no exception. It must have been October time when we embarked on a ship to bring us back to the UK. As we pulled away from the coast of Italy, I remember seeing Mount Etna with snow on top and a slight column of smoke coming from its top.

Our ship joined a convoy out at sea and we steamed in lines, heading for Gibraltar. The sea started getting rough, so I made friends with the hospital staff. Why? Well, the ship's hospital is always in the centre of the ship as it gets less movement there from bad weather. Also, there is a room, a padded cell, that is rarely used and is very comfortable. I helped the nurse in charge during the day and he let me use this room at night to sleep. The room itself was soundproof and no storm was violent enough to bother you.

On deck, guide lines had been rigged up to enable anyone to move about without fear of being thrown overboard. As we stood there watching the other ships making heavy weather of the rough seas, a cry went up. Several ships had barrage balloons attached as protection from enemy aircraft and one had broken loose. It was from a ship ahead of us and it came bouncing between the lines of ships. It really did bounce: first, it would hit the sea, then rise high in the air. The last we saw of it was when it was heading back along the Mediterranean at great speed.

9

Dear Old Blighty

The ship entered the River Clyde on its way to let us disembark at the port of Glasgow. It was a great feeling to be returning home after sixteen months away. We docked and the first thing was the arrival on board of the Customs officers who went through our kit very carefully indeed. We thought it was a bit much: we had been fighting for our country but were not to be allowed a few extra fags on the side. One lad, who had quite a bit extra, carried it up to the deck and threw it overboard but still had to pay for the excess. The Customs men stood at the bottom of the gangway when we got off the ship though they soon moved after being firmly nudged by some of the lads. We formed up and marched off to catch a train to go down south to Bury St Edmunds where we were to be stationed.

It was evening when we arrived at our new camp and we quickly settled in and went to bed. We were given a late call the next day and spent the rest of the morning having a look around the camp. It was a pleasant place and not all that far from the town.

I was called to the office and told my transfer to Airborne had come through, but leave was shortly to be granted. If I was to be transferred I would have to forego my leave and immediately join a squad to go to Hardwick Hall. I made a quick decision and agreed to go right away. A hectic hour and I was packed again. I was issued with travel warrant and directions. With quick cheerios all round, I was off again. Hardwick Hall was the home of the Airborne forces and it was not far from my home town of Sheffield – only about 20 miles away.

At Hardwick Hall we did some very hard training including physical exercise and route marches, during which we ran uphill and marched down, carrying lots of equipment. There was a friendly atmosphere among the men and we helped each other through the training. If one man found it hard, another would take his rifle and someone else would carry his pack until he had recovered.

You never walked anywhere inside the camp: as soon as you came out of a hut, you doubled. From Hardwick Hall we moved to Ringway for our parachute training. Everything went well – I jumped from a balloon in daylight and did six jumps out of a Whitley aircraft (nicknamed 'flying coffins'). We also jumped from a balloon on a dark, wet night – it was a real stinker but we made it all right.

We were presented with our 'wings' at a ceremony in a big hall and were given the full treatment. We sang ribald songs and gave lots of cheers for our instructors. When we left the hall to get our wings stitched on to our jackets we were told that we could go into Manchester for a night out. When we got on the buses everyone was trying to get a seat on the left-hand side so that the wings on your right shoulder were showing. It was a good feeling.

I went back with the rest of the squad to a camp at a place called Larkhill and word came through from 30 Corps that I was to stay there. My first impression of Larkhill was that it was very bleak and not up to much.

Christmas 1943 was spent at home in Sheffield and I had a very good time. My two sisters were at home. One was in the WAAF and the other was a cook at Rampton Prison. My brother was there as well. He had lost his wife a few months previously. There were also my brother's three daughters whom my mother was looking after. We had a great time and it was very noisy. I met up with many old friends during my Christmas leave, some of whom had not been out of England since returning from Dunkirk.

Returning to Larkhill, I soon settled into the routine that most infantry men are familiar with – parades, drill, weapon training, physical exercise and the odd jump here and there. I became accustomed to flying over Dumbbell Wood and Netheravon. There was never a dull moment. I enjoyed the route marches and the drill.

It must have been about April 1944 that 30 Corps required my services again, but I told my Larkhill mates I would be back with them as soon as possible. As I travelled about from one division to another, I could see preparations were being made and something would be happening soon. Tanks and armoured cars were stacked alongside every road down south and there was little room for anything else. My officer took me to one side and explained that he would be going with a driver and radio operator in a glider with 6th Airborne. Now I knew why I had been rushed into passing my parachute course. I was to drop with the 13th Parachute Battalion and meet him at Divisional HQ. Not knowing how things would work out over there, they would also take a motorcycle for me to use in case that was the only way to keep in touch with 30 Corps HQ.

I was taken back to rejoin the Airborne at Larkhill in Wiltshire. There were huge piles of goods stacked in fields and a number of guns and tanks. The following day I went to Bulford to meet some men from the 5th Parachute Brigade. They were Royal Signals men whom I might have had to get in touch with once we had landed.

Towards the end of May we concentrated in a camp not far from an airfield that we were to take off from. Once there, no one was allowed out of the camp and we had many sessions in which we discussed various tactics we might employ if certain things happened. Arms and ammunition were to be divided among us to carry on the drop. We had a little light relief in fixing up a boxing ring in which there were several fights: it passed the time.

We were taken to the airfield where gliders were being loaded with vehicles and motor cycles. Everyone was busy doing something. Men who were to parachute were getting their equipment ready for the drop. For them it was to be a night drop and it was a big help to have a kitbag containing arms and ammunition on a nylon rope, so it could be lowered and the touch felt before landing. It gave a brief warning of whether you were to hit a tree, a house or the ground, which was important during the hours of darkness.

I must admit on looking back that I never doubted our ability to bring this operation to a successful conclusion. It was what we had been waiting for. On the evening of 5 June we were ready with all our gear, blackened faces, knives and grenades. Grenades were my favourite weapon. Whether priming them or making them safe, I loved it. Whenever we had been on exercises, what grenades were left over had to be made safe and I would get the men to hand them in at the edge of the camp. When they saw me get out my long pin, which I used to wear on a belt, they all rapidly disappeared. People say you should not remove a fuse with a pin but I never had any trouble.

Our officers said we would be baling out about 12.30 or 1 o'clock on the morning of 6 June and we were to make sure we got to our rendezvous. We were to stick together and to hell with anybody else. The password was *Punch* answered by *Judy*. Anything else – *Domino*.

10

Into the Unknown

It was only a short ride to the airfield. I wondered what were the thoughts of the men in my truck. I was all right, 23 years old, very fit and excited. To my Mum and Dad, I had said good-bye. I was not courting seriously and so I did not have anybody to worry about. Some of the lads had only recently married and their feelings were another matter.

We took off for Normandy in the early hours. During the flight we got a running commentary and everybody was busy checking their equipment and ensuring that they were hooked up correctly. Suddenly, it went quiet; first the red light, quickly followed by the green and we dropped out of the plane with very great speed. I do not think my feet touched anything – I just went. A 'chute tore past me. It was probably carrying ammunition and had not opened. I felt some branches catch my legs and then, whoomph, the breath was taken out of my body. 'Where the hell am I,' I thought. It was dark. I felt around and eventually found I had landed on a garden shed in the middle of an allotment.

I quickly got out of my 'chute and checked my gear. It was all present and correct. I made my way through the allotment and heard someone ahead of me. With no intention of calling out *Punch* and getting blasted off the face of the earth, I cleared the allotment and went on to a country road. At least, it looked like one in that there were hedges and ditches. I fell into a ditch and somebody said, 'Punch'. From me came the mumbled reply, 'Judy' and then came the questions. 'What the hell do you think you are doing walking all over us?' These men were

Paras, but not those I had jumped with, and they had been resting in the ditch. An officer then shouted at me for having my Sten gun slung round my neck. 'What if we had been Germans and shot you?' he asked. My reply was that we would all be dead. In each hand I was carrying a grenade with the pins out: if I had been shot at everyone would have gone to blazes. I would not have said the password to anyone. I could not lose with my grenades. The officer thought it was a good idea and that both myself and my grenades should stay with them. They were the 13th Parachute Battalion and had lost several men in the landings. I got the job of being no. 2 on the Bren gun. No. 2 carried the ammunition and took over if no. 1 was hit. We met up with other Paras and aimed for the high ground at a place called Ranville. We were warned that the Germans were in strength around the area.

We soon encountered the enemy and a ding-dong battle ensued with some casualties being sustained. As no. 2 on the Bren I had never before refilled so many cartridges. No. 1 never complained, so I must have done a reasonable job. By the end of the day we had taken the higher ground. Someone said the area was called Le Mesnil, but it is all the same when you are in a ditch stuffing rounds into magazines or running like the clappers between trees on a hillside.

We received instructions to halt and dig in. Warding off the occasional enemy patrol, who were feeling their way around, we came to the conclusion this was our patch. The 6th Air Landing Brigade gave us excellent support although when their guns were pounding the enemy's front line it was as hair-raising for us as for Jerry. We catnapped whenever we were able; it was the only way. There was a lot of activity to our left. Someone was getting some stick. I have found out since that Jerry was trying to break through at Breville, but could not do so.

Besides being no. 2 on the Bren, I was chief activator of grenades. I earned my keep, even though I did not belong to this unit; a 30 Corps bloke – there by accident. My intention was to make my way to my own unit as soon as conditions permitted. One evening two new men arrived and the platoon corporal told me to pack my gear and get on my way. I felt awful and was very much upset. 5th Parachute Brigade had all they needed from me and I was no longer required. It was not the first time I had been let down but I quickly bounced back.

6th Airborne Division HQ was situated in a big quarry close to the River Orne and a fair distance from where I had landed. I was taken there in a jeep and then picked up and taken to 30 Corps HQ on the outskirts of Bayeux which was about 25 miles away.

I was amazed at the amount of equipment stacked in the fields as we went along the main roads. There were troops everywhere and I could readily believe the statistic that 25 men are required to support one man in the front line. However, the most noticeable thing was the dreadful smell. All the cattle in the fields had been killed and they now looked like barrage balloons. When they burst, as they did, you needed a gas mask. There were enough tanks down here to start another war or two.

I arrived at 30 Corps HQ and my old officer was there. He told me that they had had a good landing in daylight and the quarry had been only a short distance away. They had enquired after me, but some of the men I had dropped with had not survived and it was thought I was also a casualty. I had a quiet time for a while, then I buttonholed my officer about my, seemingly, forgotten transfer to the Airborne Division. I had an interview with him two days later. He informed me that he had enquired how I had got on with the 13th and had received a good report. They had told him I was a good man with grenades. He then asked if I knew it was wrong to use a pin to take a fuse from a grenade. 'Of course I do, Sir,' I replied. He smiled. I would be moving over to the 5th Parachute Brigade HQ on 27 July 1944, he told me. I was delighted.

The following day, I learned that my old battalion of the Essex Regiment was moving into a farm close to where I was now stationed. I decided to take a look. They were in the process of moving in when I arrived. Regimental police were busy directing the way and as I knew many of them I had a good chat. They told me some chaps I knew had been lost and others wounded. I promised to come and see them all again and they said they would let some of my old mates know I was still alive and kicking.

There was a great deal of activity in the air. Caen had received a one thousand bomber raid and part of it had spilled over into Villiers Bocage which was not far from Bayeux. I saw the enemy shoot down several of our bombers as I went about my duties. German anti-aircraft shells explode with black smoke whereas ours do so with white. One chap I saw tried to bale out but his canopy caught the tail of the aircraft and dragged him down with it – not the best way to go.

I received a message to report to the office for my papers for the transfer to 5th Parachute Brigade. At long last. I had travelled a long way since applying for this posting and now it was here. That night I had a drink with the lads.

The next morning, I was up bright and early, no thick head and full of go. I set off in a jeep with a sergeant driving; he wanted to see what was going on in the rest of the Normandy bridgehead. There was plenty to see with all the various units moving around with their field guns and Bren carriers. It appeared we were here to stay.

As we approached the Caen area there were masses of tanks moving across the open fields near the main road that led on to the River Orne. At one of the crossroads there were officers and men with a massive blackboard, situated on the central reservation. The board had the Normandy bridgehead drawn on it with the position of all units at the front line. It was good. When positions changed, the details were amended. I had never seen this done before. Someone had a good idea.

Activity increased as we continued our journey. Officers with field glasses were stood in groups by the side of the road watching tank formations getting set up and in deep discussion. We stopped for a while to see what it was all about. It was getting close to lunchtime, so we made tracks for the quarry and 6th Airborne Division HQ. We went over Pegasus Bridge that had quickly been taken.

I reported to the orderly room and was told a jeep would be arriving from 5th Parachute Brigade to pick me up. While waiting, I chatted to some of the men and was given graphic accounts of how they landed on D-Day in their gliders. Many had been shot down and others were a day and a half late in arriving at their rendezvous – the quarry. Apparently they had had a rough time.

The jeep arrived and I met a couple of men I would be with from now on. They were both very sociable and told me not to take offence if I was helped out of the vehicle by somebody's boot; Jerry was given to mortaring the road we had to take quite often as it was the only one up to Le Mesnil from Divisional HQ. I told them it was probable I would be the first out.

We pulled up in the yard of a big farmhouse that had a number of outbuildings and I was introduced to a big cockney fellow who suggested I share his dugout. He took me to it and I placed my gear there. The walls had been lined with a parachute he had found. It looked good. He had laid some lengths of timber across the roof and piled earth on top to a depth of about two feet. 'Don't worry,' he said, 'We get mortared quite a lot but they don't come through this roof.' I was to appreciate this at a later date.

I was allotted a bike and shown around the different Battalion HQs. What a laugh we had when we went to 13th Battalion

HQ. I was asked if I wanted to come and prime some grenades for them. I was never to live that down!

The cockney lad was called Ron Smith, and we became good mates. We frequently got shelled, mortared and all the usual stuff that goes with being close to Jerry. When your own field guns were giving the Jerries near the front line a pasting, it was nearly as bad as when Jerry was giving you one.

The French people who owned the farmhouse would not move out. Our unit had the ground floor rooms and they had those upstairs. At no time did a shell or mortar bomb touch the house. Possibly they were good friends of the Germans.

After a short time things had settled down and Ron and I went to Bayeux on his bike. We spent a while looking around and then decided to go on to Villiers Bocage where, we had been told, my old battalion the Essex Regiment was situated. The road was littered with knocked-out vehicles and we were met by a solitary soldier who put his hand out to stop us. We pulled up. 'You don't want to go down there, he's down there,' he said. 'He' was Jerry, of course. We were then asked if we were 'Essex' and when we replied we were, he told us their HQ was nearby. As we rode into a clearing in the woods, a few men came out waving their arms and telling us to make less noise. I recognised most of them and when I got off the bike and removed my beret, they also recognised me. Everyone wanted to shake hands. It was just as if we had arrived home they made us so welcome.

We went on to visit the Regimental Signals platoon that was in a field behind a hedge. There were more handshakes and we were told the latest news. Many men I had known were no longer alive and one had been killed only the day before. He was a good lad, not a bit like me who was always pushing his luck. A few shells came over and we finished our conversation sprawled out in a ditch. Ron and I said cheerio and went back to our unit. It certainly had been an interesting journey.

Arriving back at our own position in the front line, we were surprised to find that things were looking up. It was possible we would be breaking out of our bridgehead in the near future. The brigade was ready for moving out. After a heavy barrage by our guns we went forward in a lane through an orchard. The lane cut right through the German front line down to a metalled road. There was a horse and cart with two German soldiers – all were dead. I think they had been supplying provisions by this method because it was quieter.

We covered a good distance that day with just the odd display of resistance by the Germans, but nothing serious. However, we did see quite a few dead Germans by the roadside. The first real resistance came when we got close to a town by the name of Pont L'Evêque. After we made our way into the town, the centre was set on fire. We were on one side of the town, the Germans were on the other and the river ran through the middle with the only bridge having been damaged. Snipers were very busy. Occasionally a girl would be caught with a sniper. One night I was going through the town centre; the buildings were ablaze and it looked a little gruesome. I came upon an engineer who had just spotted a sniper with a girl and as we watched an old lady went up to him, pulled out a revolver and shot him dead. Possibly the girl was some relation to the old lady, but I do not know for certain. I went on my way and left them to it. There was nothing I could do and, sometimes, it pays to turn a blind eye.

We were attempting to get across the damaged bridge when I was approached by a civilian who asked me to help him with a dead Para sergeant who had 'bombs' in his pocket. He looked surprised when I merely used my jack-knife and cut off the pockets. It would have been too dangerous to remove the grenades from the pockets.

I managed to clear the wreckage from part of the bridge, leaving two girders bare. They were side by side and each one was about six inches wide, giving a total width of one foot. With some difficulty I rode my bike across the river and, naturally, I like to think I was the first to cross at that particular point.

Some men were trying to cross the river further up and I thought I would see if they had managed to do so. They had crossed and Brigadier Poett (later General Sir Nigel Poett) and an escort were in a jeep. The last time the brigadier had spoken to me was when we were sheltering in a ditch near Le Mesnil. I joined them and he asked that I lead the way, which I did. We joined the main road and found the battalions. They were well advanced and doing very well. With the brigadier around they really had not much option. About three or four miles further on, the battalion was spread out on either side of the road in the ditches. In front of us, Jerry had blown the railway bridge, leaving a mound of earth about twenty feet high. It was covered from the other side by machine guns and mortars.

The brigadier ordered us into ditches and said I was to follow him if he motioned for me to do so. If he did I had to stick to him like whatever to a blanket. You most certainly earned your corn when you were escort to Brigadier Poett. Jerry was pounding us heavily with mortars and there were repeated cries for stretcher bearers. He was really lobbing them over. I watched sir very closely. I had heard he did not bother about his own skin and the rumours were right. He nodded to me and I went to him where he was stood with the commander and the adjutant of the battalion. The four of us stood there with mortar bombs dropping around us, close and within a few feet. They discussed how to overcome the problem of crossing the river. No one spoke to me. I just stood there like soft Mick. I could see faces peering out of ditches. Whether they thought I was brave or completely daft, I can only guess. The latter is more than likely.

After a while we went back to our ditches. I had no sooner got my bum settled than the adjutant came over and asked that

I ran him back to Pont L'Evêque. I drove very fast and the adjutant thought he was in the Isle of Man TT. I dropped him off and he ordered me back to the blown bridge. My return was met with guns from behind us bursting in the woods ahead of us. Clearly the return of the officer was to start this operation.

By the next morning a way had been cleared. The battalions were really moving. Evening came and we were well to the fore. A big white farmhouse was selected as a Brigade HQ. The battalions were combing the valley below. The farmhouse was hit several times and it was a little uncomfortable. Fortunately it was built of solid stone. I had to go out several times with messages and was glad of a shed near the gate in which to shelter. It was decided to dig trenches alongside the farmhouse away from the shelling. We had brought in two German prisoners and I decided they could do the digging for me.

The shelling got less intensive with only the occasional burst. However, the targeting remained fairly accurate. The digging of the ditches continued and I noticed that one of the Germans was crying. It occurred to me that he thought he was digging his own grave. I have a funny sense of humour and so kept making him lay down in the trench to make sure it was the right size. When the trenches were finished the German realised he was not for the chop and was a lot happier.

One day I was walking around the farmhouse and another chap was coming towards me. A shell came over, hit the house and exploded. I dived one way and he went the other. Unfortunately, he was dead. I was caught in the open several times. You could hear a mortar 'coughing'. That was when they were being fired and you got a move on and dived for cover. As you dived you saw the shrapnel cutting through the grass when you neared the ground and wondered how it managed to miss.

We passed through several villages and the villagers came out and hung garlands of flowers round our necks. The brigadier looked very good with his decorations. He tried to look serious but did not quite manage to do so. As we went through the villages our battalion men brought in prisoners and the French *Maquis* soldiers would strut about armed to the teeth. When the Germans were there they were nowhere to be seen but when our blokes had chased Jerry out of sight they came out in all their glory. It takes all sorts to make a world!

The French were also in the habit of shaving off girls' hair when they had been discovered associating with German soldiers. A prostitute was allowed to go to bed with a German but, if a decent girl just walked out with one she was ridiculed in this way. We thought it was rather stupid.

We arrived at a place called Pont-and-Mer. Here we had orders to clean our weapons, get washed, shaved and clean ourselves up as well as we were able. We were told we would shortly be returning to Normandy.

Before our brigade went to Arromanches, I escorted the Brigadier onto the main coast road that ran on top of the cliffs between Honfleur and the next town eastwards. The Germans fired their 'Doodlebugs' from the cliffs at this point. These devices were pilotless planes carrying explosives and were aimed at southern England. When the fuel which propelled them had been used up they would fall to earth and explode. The ramps at the launch site were very primitive – simple wooden affairs that could quickly be constructed and placed in position. The 'Doodlebugs' were stored in a man-made hill which was covered in grass and looked very natural. Railway lines, used for delivering the rockets to the store, ran alongside a road that was covered by large trees. It was extremely good camouflage. The installation had been destroyed by an air raid.

A few days' later we arrived around Arromanches. It seemed strange coming back and it was very quiet. The whole division congregated on the downs, and a big service was held in memory of those who had died or been wounded. It was a very moving occasion.

Following the service, the various units moved to the Mulberry Harbour – a man-made device that had been floated across from the UK. As you walked across the harbour it wallowed and heaved with the movement of the sea. From here we boarded lighters which took us out to Liberty ships manned by Americans. We were then taken to a larger ship that we boarded by scrambling up nets like monkeys. After boarding it was a matter of waiting until we reached the UK. On our arrival we went straight to Bulford, the home for 5th Parachute Brigade and Divisional HQ.

11

New Friends

Settling down in the Bulford camp was new to me but I soon make myself at home anywhere. First there was a bit of leave. The London trains came right into the 7th Parachute Battalion area that was just across the road – very convenient. Four of us caught the train to Waterloo and went straight to Jermyn Street where we had a Turkish bath and a massage before being thrown into a very cold pool. It was then on to the Nuffield Club where they pressed our uniforms and gave us all a haircut. We felt marvellous.

Following a night on the town and much drinking we split up to travel home. I arrived in Sheffield the next evening and found it very quiet after the events of the previous months. After seeing my family and friends and letting them see I was alive and well, I reluctantly returned to my unit in Bulford.

Ron Smith and I were firm friends by now, and he took me home with him to Deptford in the east end of London. His family was good to me and I felt at home in their company. Some nights we would go to the 'dogs' at Catford. It was good fun. I always backed on the Tote and my favourite numbers were 2-4 up and down. Usually, I managed to come out with a few quid. One Saturday night both Ron and I were a bit short of the readies. Ron's Dad was going to the Greenwich Baths where they were staging boxing matches. For a good fight we earned ten shillings. A good crowd was in attendance and they threw in to the ring a few extra coins, so we did quite well.

Each year Ron's family went hop-picking. That year, Ron and I went with them and it was great fun. We worked in the fields and stayed on the farm in the barns at a place called Knockolt. Each evening there were drinks, dancing and singing.

When we returned to our unit we were engaged in military exercises on the hills around Bulford. There was a big quarry here that was used for firing our Sten guns. Figures would pop up here and there, and we made it a competition to see who was the best. Some men practised with grenades picked up in France; one went off unexpectedly, killing one man and severely wounding several others. I was in the party of six that took the dead man's body home to his family by train. We stayed for the funeral. He was buried with full military honours and it was a very emotional experience.

We carried on with our various training schemes. This included route marches. We ran up hills and marched down and covered a great deal of ground. Some of our men would dress as German soldiers, pretend to drop at night and lay waste to the countryside. They were caught all over the place including Winchester. It was all good practice. Some men actually walked around Piccadilly Circus dressed as German soldiers and no one paid them the least attention. There were so many different uniforms about that not many people could identify them correctly. Our motorcycles were stamped with the German eagle to make them look more authentic.

As the year neared its end, and Christmas drew close, we all thought of going home. A friend of mine had a Riley sports car which he kept in a garage in Bulford. He came from Manchester; it was arranged I would get the petrol and on Christmas Eve we would set off with me driving as far as Sheffield and then him continuing to his home. Unfortunately, it was not to be.

12

Off to the Ardennes

NCOs were dashing about with instructions for us to get our gear together. We were on our way again and had to be ready to move by 9 o'clock that evening – Christmas Eve. My friend's car was filled with petrol and our leave was cancelled. Everything happened very fast and by the next morning we were unloading the ship at Ostende. Men on motorcycles were made responsible for controlling the convoy on the long trip to the Ardennes and ensuring no vehicle lagged behind.

Ron was acting as escort to our company officer. The previous time he carried out escort duty was on D-Day when the officer was killed in the fighting as they made their way through hedgerows in Normandy. We managed to get to Brussels and were on target for arrival at our destination by the evening. My motorcycle then got a puncture that took me a long time to mend because it was so cold. By the time I had completed the repairs I was both cold and hungry, and so I decided to stop at a little village cafe for a bite to eat. After an excellent meal of egg and chips, I had a cigarette and a chat with the lady who served me. I then got my gear together and left the premises. Almost immediately, I was jumped on by three men who put a rope around my neck. I cursed and swore so loudly I was probably heard for many a mile – I have a loud voice. They then threw the other end of the rope over a lamp post and heaved; I continued to play merry hell until I was starting to lose consciousness when a jeep drew up nearby. A number of white-helmeted Americans with big truncheons got out and cleared a path, hitting out at all the spectators. I thought,

'Oh no, I'm not going to be saved by Yanks.' But I was. They cut me down and I landed in the gutter, unable to speak and with a sore throat. The Yankee sergeant then told me a group of German soldiers had been making their way back to Germany through the Ardennes. With me in camouflage uniform and a motorcycle with the German eagle on, the natives thought I was a German and had decided to put me six feet under. I nodded my thanks and tried to smile but could not make a very good job of it.

I continued with my journey and did not stop until I saw a farmhouse with English vehicles parked outside. The men there belonged to a light armoured brigade which would be with the 6th Airborne. It was getting dark by then. I had a meal with them and they let me sleep in the back of one of their wagons. They treated me very well and the next morning I had a good breakfast. Their officer said that Namur, where I was heading, was only about 25 kilometres away and suggested I went along with his lads as they knew the location of the enemy. The Germans were across a valley that was too deep for tanks to attempt a crossing. I stayed with them until lunchtime, having spent the morning riding in one of their tanks. The lads filled my bike with fuel and I was in Namur in no time. I reported to my unit and explained about my puncture but not the attempted hanging. They were pleased I had made it and straight away sent me out on a job with the Yanks who were close by.

Early the next morning, the unit paraded and made its way up into the Ardennes. It had begun to snow and stayed that way. The Ardennes was very different from what we were used to, with its many tall pine trees. Our battalions were fighting their way through the trees and over the hills and recaptured land previously taken by the Germans. We were continually on the move and I just happened to see an old English newspaper that told how the Americans had taken the town we had only recently left. This could not be true. The only Americans in the area were many dead ones in the forests who had been cut down when the Germans had attacked and gone right through.

Leaving the town we went through the forests. I have never before or since seen trees as tall or in such numbers. There was evidence of the Americans retreating as we came across blown bridges of little consequence. I could jump across these rivers. They were not well versed in this type of warfare.

The brigade searched all over for the Germans but they seemed to have done a vanishing act. We went back onto the roads. As we came downhill on a long twisting road, platoons were sent up side roads to see if anyone was there. Near the bottom of the main road, one platoon went into a village by the name of Bure and got a pasting. The Germans were there, and by the fire power there were a lot of them. Reinforcements were quickly drafted in and the 13th Battalion gave Jerry some stick but had difficulty getting much further than the centre of the village which was on fire. Later we learned that the 13th Battalion had come up against a Panzer Group – the equivalent of a brigade in our army. They were also equipped with Tiger tanks.

Our tanks tried an attack on the Germans in the centre of Bure but it was a disaster and twenty of our tanks were put out of action in as many seconds. There was no shortage of anti-tank guns in the German army. I saw all this from a vantage point on a village road. It was a shambles, but Jerry could not make anything out of it as the 13th Battalion held fast. Jerry was very good at turning nothing into something given a half chance. The reason for this, I think, was that he gave full responsibility to his senior NCOs to take over command should the officers be killed. We could, I think, have learned from this practice.

Inside the house that held the Battalion HQ were men who were firing from upstairs. I went down to the cellar where some of the wounded were waiting for nightfall before being evacuated. Others were grouped round a table on which there was a radio transmitter and receiver in contact with Brigade HQ. There was also Mary, a big cow belonging to the owners of the property. A side door from the cellar led to the outside but the cow could not be let out because of the fighting. You could hardly see in the cellar for the smoke and Mary decided to mess all over the table which included the radio set. Amid the laughter, we did our best to clean the radio but it was never the same again.

When it was getting dark and snowing hard, I took a couple of lads in a jeep to Brigade HQ and left them with the medics. The jeep did not have automatic windscreen washers and I had to use my left hand to clear the snow; this was not easy. Before leaving HQ, I had a shower and got my uniform cleaned; I felt like a new man.

The 13th Battalion pulled out at night. Our guns went into action for what seemed like hours and another division followed. Jerry had vanished without trace. He was exceptionally clever at knowing when to call it a day. In my opinion, the 13th Battalion had done very well indeed in holding a much superior force in numbers of men and tanks and they had not conceded an inch. They were good lads.

We were not needed any more in this area and we were given orders to make tracks to Holland. We went in convoy which made good time without any breakdowns or punctures. It was an uneventful trip.

13

Holland

As the convoy entered Holland, I was asked by our officer to escort a truck to Eindhoven. We travelled to a railway yard where large trucks laden with coal were entering. They had to drive over rails and as they did so coal was thrown off onto the road and children with bags, buckets and baskets collected as much as they could carry. I remembered doing the same thing during the General Strike of 1926. We kids were the saviour of our households in those days. The only difference was that our local police chased us and, if we were caught, the coal was taken from us and there would be no fire at home that night. No one chased these Dutch children.

From Eindhoven we returned to our division. Nearby to where 5th Brigade HQ was temporarily stationed was a sort of monastery where one priest had been left in charge; a more miserable bloke I have never met. I do not think he had ever smiled in his life. We visited this place and went through it like a dose of salts. In the lofts we found loads of big hams hanging from the roof. Being soldiers and always hungry, we just took a few. The priest took a very dim view of the situation and ranted and raved over a motley crowd of hooligans pinching his food. At least that is what we thought he was saying!

He reported us to our officers and acted the injured party extremely well. I almost admired his poise and posturing as to how he was on his last legs in respect of food. He certainly did not look underfed with his heavy jowls and fat belly. Anyway, he convinced our officer. Being a man of the cloth helped him, I suppose. Our company had to compensate him with the equivalent of two days' rations. That was the verdict of our officer. We had to eat the hams instead of saving them for a rainy day. A bit much, I thought, two whole days' rations.

Even so, we could see the funny side of it. One of our men was an artist on a local paper back home. He drew a picture of our boys on a large sheet of paper. You could distinguish the various individuals. On the front row were five pigs' heads in place of human faces. It was easy to see who the five culprits were. The cartoon was good and had the caption, 'who's pinched the hams?' It was put on the notice board outside the office and someone saw our officer laughing his head off in his office.

We survived; some Dutch families invited us into their homes. They had only meagre rations and mainly lived on cabbage soup, but were willing to share what little they had with us. On one occasion we organised a visit to some town about ten or so miles away where there was a NAAFI. We had made a collection of money from the lads and bought chocolate, cakes, bread, butter and all sorts of other treats, which we distributed among the families who had treated us so well. It was a pleasure to see their faces. We were lucky to be able to return their favours.

Our battalions in the line were in full view of the enemy and so things had to be done during the hours of darkness. We went up and down a nearby hill at night like yo-yos. One night when we were returning to base, the sentry must have dozed off because when we passed there was no challenge. He usually called out; this time nothing. A few yards further on and a shot blasted between the driver of the jeep and myself, leaving a hole in the dashboard. The sentry must have woken up as we passed and let fly. We collected the RSM and returned to give him a right roasting. I expected to get shot at by the enemy, but not by our own men. The sentry got a rollicking and was dispatched to one of the forward companies so that he could practice his shooting on the Germans.

Each morning, a German would get up on the river bank in PT kit and go through a series of exercises in full view of everybody. No one ever took a shot at him; we just had a good laugh.

One night a couple of Germans were caught swimming down the river. It had been their intention to blow up a bridge near Venlo about twelve miles away. They were big men – arrogant and very full of themselves. Instead of climbing over gates they would vault over them. I got the job of taking them back to Brigade HQ. They would not talk and no one managed to get a word out of them. A decision to move them to a place where they would face heavy questioning was taken. We were having some very cold weather, and walking about all night on a tennis court covered with gravel, without clothing or foot-wear, made them eager to tell everything they knew. A bucket or two of cold water thrown over them also helped. These men belonged to a German parachute division who were in the area across the river from us. It would seem they had done no damage.

A latrine had been dug for us, by some men from the Pioneer Corps, just inside the woods at the back of the monastery. They also dug a large pit for sanitation purposes and placed a single plank across it to sit on. It was precarious and, inevitably, there were several mishaps. The stench was unbelievable. Life was not easy.

The woods at the back of the monastery stretched for miles and contained wild pigs. Our officer got the bright idea that we should go and catch some. I was one of the men chosen. He asked to take a Bren gun! Whether he intended it for use on a pig or any Germans we ran across, I do not know and he did not say. However, on that occasion we saw neither pigs nor Germans.

At that time things were very quiet on our part of the front. One night, we had to take a couple of men to do a job for the Independent Company which was located further up the river. The hill behind us followed the course of the river. We were told to be careful when we reached the rise behind where the Independent Company's billets where situated. On our side of the hill the headlamps could be used occasionally but had to be turned off before we topped the rise or Jerry would get you when reaching near the bottom of the river. He could time it very well. We were at the top of the hill almost before we realised it and we were concerned whether we had put the lights out in sufficient time.

With the engine cut off, we went quietly down the hill and approached a large square facing the river. The jeep was hidden behind a dilapidated store. We then ran across to the ruins of a church, which was a heap of very large stones. The company had its HQ deep in the cellars of the church. Jerry's timing was good. He sprayed bullets across the square. We went in all directions and I ended up in an oil drum. It is amazing how you react when you see that bloke with the big scythe coming! The ricochets were worse than the rounds which I believed came from a 42–34 infantry machine gun. About a thousand rounds a minute they were capable of – much faster than a Bren. I waited and waited. Several times I nearly went but stayed. Eventually, throwing caution to the winds, I went and just made it to the cellar. Everyone was grinning as I went in. They had seen me go into the oil drum. Luckily, they had managed to get behind one of the large stones of the former church and then dashed across the square. I did not feel comfortable sitting in an oil drum but I survived. Jerry continued shelling; I think he was after our jeep. I crept outside but the action was too fierce to consider going any further. It was also snowing heavily. Before leaving Brigade HQ, our officer had said we were to try and be back before the following morning for 'a fit Para exam'.

Returning to the cellar, I had a cup of tea with the lads. The two men whom Ron and I had brought out had repaired the radio set that was giving trouble and so we were ready for off. Jerry had quietened down and we thought we would risk moving off. We tried, but when we reached the jeep we found it had two flat tyres. They were ripped to shreds – from ricochets, I presumed. Back in the cellar, I enquired whether it was safe to go down the river back to our HQ. They said there would be no difficulty getting us through their lines, but beyond there was open swampy land. Nobody knew if it was mined.

The snow was thick by this time and I thought it would be a help if we decided to walk along the bank of the river. It was too far to walk on the roads. I asked the men if they wished to come with Ron and myself. We had decided to take a chance on the open land not being mined. I explained my plan to them and stressed that things might go wrong. The men decided to come along with Ron and me. Getting to the edge of the company's area proved not to be a problem. Ron and I decided to take it in turns to take the lead. As the lead man walked forward, the others walked behind in his footprints. This was the benefit of there being snow on the ground.

That is the way we made it back to our unit. There was nothing new in this method. Lots of soldiers have been obliged to do the same sort of thing. When you were leading you did feel a little queasy. In North Africa, I was on a similar journey when the lead man put his foot on an 'S' mine. When stepped on, this mine detonated and the explosion caused a canister to be thrown six feet in the air. There were over 300 half-inch ball bearings inside these canisters and they could, and did, cause much damage. This man kept his foot on the mine and, to save us, he lost his leg. It is not funny by any means.

On our way back we went through a seemingly deserted village and could not see a sentry anywhere. I went up to what I thought was the village hall and quietly opened the door. It was daylight by this time. The sentry was crouched in a corner of the vestibule between the two pairs of doors. I opened the inner door into the main hall and there was the whole company sound asleep, including officers and senior NCOs. I was tempted to open up with my sten gun but remembered that sentry who took a pot shot at us as soon as he awoke. Instead I wrote a note on a piece of paper – 'Kilroy was here,' it read. I could have upset the apple cart but I did not. I had been an infantryman myself and sometimes had been at the end of my tether. 'Let him who is without sin cast the first stone.'

We arrived back at HQ before midday. I explained what had gone on and offered to take two wheels to replace those which were damaged on the jeep. The officer accepted my offer and that night Ron and I went back to change the wheels. This time there were no problems.

After returning once again to HQ we had a good long sleep, after which we felt much better. The next night we went off to where the 13th Battalion was stationed. They were due to move to a new position to our right. Each night the Airborne RASC took ammunition supplies by jeep to the various battalions wherever they were located at a particular time. These men did a splendid job. No unit can fight without ammunition.

I liked visiting the 13th. Although I only knew a few men there they always made me welcome. Their CO had a very nice dog and he often took it for walks. I used to return from the 13th by going over the hills. On the top were situated the Canadians who had been supplied with some new mortars. These weapons were larger than ours. When the Canadians knew I was ex-infantry they let me have a go. I enjoyed using these powerful weapons.

When I returned to Brigade HQ, I learned everyone was to have 'a fit Para exam'. The medical centre was nearby and we had a thorough examination to make sure we were in a good condition for a forthcoming operation. We were not told what it was to be and there were all sorts of weird and wonderful ideas floating around. We were very excited and raring to have another go at Jerry.

It was very cold indeed and each morning we would greet each other with a remark such as, 'My word, are you still alive? Glad I don't live in Russia!' One evening we were told that the Americans were going to relieve us the following day. It was usual to finish an operation with a drink and a few songs around a blazing fire and that night was no exception. It was a good evening. Volunteers did turns; there were good singers and actors in our unit and a good laugh was had by everybody.

During the nights we frequently heard many heavy bombers flying over and the next morning the area would be littered with silver foil (or 'window' as it was nicknamed) which the planes had dropped to put enemy radar off their track. At Kassell there was a searchlight on the hill overlooking the River Maas. Each evening it was switched on, illuminating the area. We thought it helped the enemy as much as ourselves and often said so.

I watched the Americans roll up. There were six men to each jeep with all their gear. The cooks set up four mobile kitchens in front of the monastery – not for them one cookhouse between all units. All the cooks wore tall hats and the smell of cooking was great. No doubt the local priest was over-joyed at their arrival. Over the hill, where it had been deserted during the day, all had changed. American trucks drove about all over the place and parked in fields a short distance from the river. We could not believe what was happening. Jerry was very quiet; just watching and waiting for the opportunity to open up.

That day was one of the longest I ever lived through, just waiting for the inevitable to happen. The way these Americans went about their duties was difficult to understand; you would have thought the war was over. As evening came and it turned darker, the front line troops changed over with our unit following on after others of our troops. It was approaching 10 p.m. and we had marched about two miles along the road when all hell let loose. Our hearts went out to the Americans who had been so brash as to give Jerry all the help they could. The German gunfire was intense and heavy losses were inflicted. When we were there, each side respected the other and there was no call for showing off. We were picked up by transport, taken to the nearest port and back to England and Bulford.

14

Back in England

Settling down in our barracks at Bulford was very pleasant. Back into the old routine, it was amazing how quickly life got back into a familiar pattern. Almost immediately, we started training in parachuting techniques. We went on a practice drop – somewhere in the south – I cannot remember where, but we had the usual good night out the evening before, in that lovely place, Cambridge. We had a drink or two and got slightly inebriated. Some students complained about not being able to park their bicycles because of our presence. We found them a place; up in the trees.

The morning after the night out we tumbled out of our beds and everything was in a shambles. We made it – eventually. It was raining heavily on the airfield and there were puddles on the tarmac runways. A truck came round with our parachutes. The men inside threw them out in a nonchalant manner. We caught them whenever we could, but mine fell into a puddle. The parachutes were made of silk which when damp sticks together. I wanted mine to open and will never forget the chap who threw my parachute into the water.

We clambered into the Dakota and found that repairs were necessary to the static lines. Cotter pins were missing. This was an American plane and the chap who was to despatch us had to go round with wire and a pair of pliers to fasten the lines safely. 'Sorry, you guys,' he said 'we ain't had time to keep this plane in proper nick, but you will be OK.' After we had gone through the routine of playing hell with the pilot, telling him to stop messing about and to get the apology of an aircraft into the air, we took off. The American was not amused. He bounced the plane all over the airfield and we gave him a big cheer when we eventually became airborne. The chap who was despatching us was grinning from ear to ear. He said, 'It's a goddam pleasure to meet you guys.'

When the green light went on, we flew out. It is the only way to go. Only once, when I was learning, had I crept out and been held against the plane by the slipstream. There I was straining to get away with someone inside the plane trying to push me with their feet. It seemed to take a long time standing to attention in mid-air.

I was drifting down and enjoying the view, the weather had improved, when suddenly I heard what all paratroopers dread; the loud flapping of a parachute which has failed to open. It came past me creating an air disturbance that swung me round like a top. I watched it go down. It was a canister used for carrying arms, about eight feet long and quite large in circumference. I saw it land between two men in the dropping zone and throw up a lot of earth as though it were a bomb. I could only imagine the language used by the two paras involved. I later saw it buried in the ground some two or three feet.

Beyond the dropping zone there was a factory and all the girls who worked there waved and cheered as we landed. It must have been a pleasant surprise for them to see the operation. It was also pleasant for us to be cheered. After this exercise we returned to Bulford and everyone seemed satisfied with the outcome.

Our unit was granted a long week-end's leave. It was too far to go home to Sheffield and so I went home with Ron. On the Saturday night we had the usual drinking session. Ron's old man danced on the table and we did handstands while drinking pints of beer – not easy. The men finished the evening playing brag and pontoon. At 5 o'clock in the morning Ron and I wandered down Deptford High Street looking for a cafe where we could get some fags.

We returned to Ron's place, had a wash and a shave and then some breakfast. When we had rested for a while, Ron's Dad got the gloves out and the men all had a go. It was good fun.

Some of Ron's family saw us off at Waterloo railway station on our way back to camp. We got into barracks about 1 o'clock on the Monday morning. The remainder of that week was very hectic. The division prepared for a drop into Germany. Everything had to be ready for a last big push to end the war in Europe.

It was another chance for a good drink and lots of singing. You could feel the adrenaline flowing – this would be it.

15

Over the Rhine

We left Bulford early in the morning for the long drive to Bury St Edmunds. It was nightfall as we arrived at a place called Shepherds Grove. When everybody was inside the camp, a barrier was set up. No one was allowed in or out. Newspapers were dropped at the gate. We had our own NAAFI that was only a tent but served our purposes. Much of our time was spent getting our gear ready, making bombs and sharpening knives. We also had a boxing match.

Ron and I were told we would be going by glider. At our briefing we learned the drop would be on a place called Hamminkeln and were warned of the danger of power lines and lots of trees. We carefully memorised all the details. After the briefing, I bought a newspaper which carried a map almost identical to the one we had been studying. Apparently, the one in the paper indicated the place the Germans expected we would drop. It was not a comforting thought but we anticipated that the enemy would be waiting for us.

The following morning it was just becoming light as we climbed into trucks for the journey to the airfield. A 'Doodle-bug' was passing overhead, making a 'put-putting' noise as it did so. We thought, 'Make the most of it, Jerry, as you ain't got much time left.' Such were the feelings of myself and many others at that particular time.

The airfield was very busy. There were rows and rows of gliders and Stirling bombers awaiting our arrival. The noise was deafening as the planes took to the air towing their gliders. As soon as one pair – plane and glider – was in place ready to take off another would follow behind. It felt good to be part of such a large and important operation. Our turn came; with a deafening roar we began our run to clear the ground, belting like the clappers, when the plane towing us slewed off the runway – our plane had a punctured tyre. The mechanics fitted another tyre, we rejoined the queue and, eventually, we took off to join our mates in the air.

We were soon over the Channel, heading for Holland and the Rhine. Through small windows – probably three inches in diameter -we managed to see some bomb damage from earlier raids by our aircraft. Nearing the Rhine, the ground became obscured by smoke and not much could be seen from the air. The plane left the glider and it suddenly became strangely quiet. In the glider there were four of us sat at the tail-end – two on each side. We were then strafed by *'Ack-Ack'* fire. Holes appeared through the floor of the glider and I thought we were about to be cut in half. However, we made an almost perfect 'pancake' landing and then set about unloading the jeep and my motorcycle. We could hear a lot of firing and it appeared we had landed among a lot of Jerries. I went on my bike to investigate and had only gone a short distance through the woods when all hell broke loose. Some rounds of a machine gun hit the motorcycle and I was thrown into the undergrowth. I tried to get back to the glider but ran into several Germans who had it surrounded. It seemed we all were about to be taken prisoner and so I made myself scarce. I was later to discover that Ron and the other two had, in fact, been taken prisoner and it was to be about six months before I saw Ron again.

Hamminkeln was the place where our unit was to rendezvous. I made my way through the woods using the noise of planes to give me a sense of direction. Many of our men had got entangled in trees and were shot dead as they hung there. Coming out of the forest, I saw many casualties, some dead, some still alive. One doctor had a horse and cart and was picking up the living. There was not much he could do for those already dead. American parachutists had also dropped in our area. They had landed in batches of twenty or so, and been gunned down as they left their planes. Like ourselves, they had landed close to machine gun nests. I saw houses that had collapsed with gliders on top of them. Several gliders had caught fire with very few, if any, of the men they were carrying surviving the ordeal.

I reached my destination with 5th Parachute Brigade. MT men offered to go with me to pick up my motorcycle and we found it in the undergrowth. The men patched it up but we did not find any sign of my mates. It was a time when I did a lot of thinking but it did not help one iota. I felt very low for a few days.

The trench I was using faced thick woodland in which the Germans had strong positions with tanks at their rear. Typhoon aircraft acted as our artillery and rocketed the enemy almost continuously. By the evening of my first day in this area, we were surrounded by columns of black smoke that came from the tanks which had been destroyed. However, the Germans were also very good with their artillery and throughout the night there were constant barrages of artillery from the Reichswald forest. The following morning the platoon sergeant and myself combed the area and collected identity tags from the dead. It was not a pleasant task but one that was necessary for several reasons. The Typhoons continued their assault: they would fire their rockets about a mile or so behind us and they would scream over our heads, landing in the woods ahead of us, only a short distance away. Jerry would reply with his 88mm *Ack-Ack* artillery. I only witnessed the bringing down of one of our planes – the pilot landing nearby.

A medical hospital had been opened in a barn and also a small cemetery for those who had been killed. Sadly, our unit had men in both places and many were mates of mine. I lost friends in the Middle East and in Europe – not a subject on which I like to dwell for too long, but which is always at the back of your mind.

My third day at Hamminkeln saw the arrival of the first contingent of tanks that were to take over our position. It was a pleasant sight. Shortly afterwards the infantry arrived: they carried their machine guns in prams that they had acquired on the way. It was the first time I had seen this done. The carrying of Brens and mortars was a task which I had done more than my fair share of. Base plates for a three-inch mortar weighed sixty pounds and were difficult to manhandle over distances; *wheels* would have been very handy indeed!

We moved out but were still in a forested area. Mortar bombs would hit the branches of the trees and shower you with shrapnel and timber. My mates and I were in a 15cwt truck, going through the woods, when a bomb hit a tree above and showered us with shrapnel. One of my mates was hit all down his back but I was not hit at all. We took him to a First Aid Post and, fortunately, he survived. It was all a matter of luck. Back in England, four of us ran a bridge school – I was now the only survivor. We also had bets on how long we would survive with the one who remained alive the longest winning the kitty. Many of us, including myself, carried a hand gun in case we were unlucky and lost a limb in action. Of course, if you were to have woken up in hospital it would have been different; you would have had no choice.

As we travelled on our way, I would occasionally call at a farm and help myself to eggs, ham, bottled fruit or whatever was available. I was not fussy. Once I went into a farm early in the morning and sat down at a massive table with the whole family of fourteen or fifteen. No one spoke a word during the meal. It was a good breakfast for which I thanked them. As I was leaving, one of the old ladies gave me a few eggs – she spoke to me in English. You were not always welcome at these farms. On one I visited the farmer was terrified when I arrived for a meal and afterwards the reason became apparent. Looking round his cowsheds, I found six German soldiers who were hiding. I disarmed them and threw their rifles, minus the bolts, into a nearby pond. After searching them I marched them away and handed them over to an officer who seemed delighted to have some prisoners. His shouting at them could, probably, be heard in the German lines scarcely a mile away.

Sometimes, when men got out of concentration camps they looked around for farmhouses which they occupied. This caused a great deal of trouble and after I encountered one farm which had been taken over in this manner, I became more careful in my search for food. There must have been fifty or more men and women in this farmhouse and I was carried shoulder high and regarded as one of their saviours. At the first opportunity I left, not wishing to play the role of hero. (Later, back in England, I met one of these men and we worked together for the same firm.) For a time, I let someone else do the searching for food.

The battalions continued to pressurise the enemy. Our rest periods consisted of ten minutes curled up somewhere and then it was back to the war again. When the brigade came to a stop for an overnight job of clearing Jerry out of a village, our tanks would be called into the area. We often came across tanks that were waiting to go into action. The men would ask us for details of what could be expected and for our assessment of Jerry's strength. We would casually reply that it was OK, but that they had several SP guns which were a menace. Tank men disliked SP guns and we liked to humour them. They, of course, would retaliate with their own wry comments, in an attempt to needle us. It was all part of the game. The following day we were near Osnabruck, the sun was shining and the battalions were in the process of scouring farm buildings for enemy soldiers. I found eight Germans and an officer in one place. After searching them and disposing of their weapons in a pond, I handed them over to some of the tank men who were collecting prisoners. I gave them the bolts from the rifles but kept the officer's hand gun for myself.

Later there was a disturbance at a nearby farm building. With several other men, I jumped onto a tank and we went to investigate. I remember our tank going round the corner of the farmhouse and seeing an SP gun located inside a partially demolished building. There then came a strange sensation of 'flying' and nothing else. I did not feel too good and came round very slowly. All that I could hear were voices speaking in German. Unsure of my whereabouts, or my condition, it was some time before I opened my eyes. I could not feel my right arm or right leg. A quick look showed there was no blood and that cheered me up a little. I thought this must be a German hospital with everyone, seemingly, speaking in German. One chap saw me looking around and he shouted to someone across the hall. A nurse came over and said to me, 'So you have come round.' I was then told that I had been brought in during the afternoon with some wounded Germans. For some reason, I was thought to be one of them; maybe it was the hand gun I had acquired.

I was examined by a doctor. It was awkward undressing me but they managed. It was decided that my injuries resulted from blast and I would be all right in a few weeks. A 9mm round had entered my right leg which required attention and for which it would be necessary to travel back to Holland for treatment. They applied a strapping and gave me injections of penicillin. The following morning's breakfast consisted of a boiled egg and another shot of penicillin. I was then put into an ambulance with three other wounded men. One had been shot in the thigh, another had injuries from a mine and the third had been wounded in much the same manner as myself. However, his injuries were far worse than mine and he looked very poorly. There was not much talking throughout the journey apart from the medic travelling with us who gave a running commentary on what was happening outside.

The ambulance was obliged to make several stops and detours due to heavy traffic on the roads chasing the retreating Germans. Vehicles travelling in the opposite direction did not have the slightest chance of reaching their destination by road. There were, however, railway lines and, at least until the traffic thinned, we made use of them. After what seemed an eternity of bumps, bumps and more bumps, on the lines, we at last managed to return to the roads and pulled up by an ancient castle where we were to stay for the night. The four patients were lifted out of the ambulance and taken into a large room where we had a cup of tea and something to eat. We were then carried to the top of the castle by way of a winding staircase. As we approached the top we heard the sound of flapping wings – many of them. They must have been big bats although we did not see them. We slept well, probably due to the injections given to us. In the morning, we had to make the return journey down the winding stairs – very difficult it proved to be: I expected to fall off the stretcher at any time. The nurses were all men who were very good at giving injections and seeing we were well fed.

I am sorry to say that the chap who had injuries similar to mine did not live through the night and another patient took his place for the next part of our journey in the ambulance. The equipment being carried by road continued to be very heavy and again we were obliged to make use of the railway tracks. I still had no feeling in my arm and leg and was given further injections by one of the medics. We stopped for the night at a very nice place by the river where we were given a warm reception. Here the nurses were all female which was a pleasant change. There were no bats about that night.

On the following day we called in at a hospital somewhere

in the Reichswald forest area so that doctors could carry out examinations. A young doctor tried to get some reaction from my right arm and my injured leg without any success. We stayed there overnight. It was interesting that German nurses were also attending to British patients. We were told to be prepared for long delays as we approached the bridge over the River Rhine on the next stage of our journey.

This warning proved to be no exaggeration. As we neared the Rhine, we joined a long queue. According to our medic, the Americans were crossing the bridge with trucks and masses of equipment in a convoy that appeared to have no end. After only a short wait, we were allowed to cross – possibly we were given priority because of our vehicle being an ambulance. The medic continued his commentary throughout the rest of the journey: in Goch nothing was left standing above two feet high, very bleak to say the least – whoever was here had certainly suffered. The description went on until we crossed the River Maas. We were then in Venlo nearing the hospital to which we had been sent. It was dark when the ambulance pulled in at the back of the hospital. The medics carried the four of us, on our stretchers, into the courtyard and handed us over to the hospital staff. We said our thanks and good-byes to the medics and wished them all the best. The medic who had been responsible for looking after my arm and leg told me that my medical notes had been handed to a nursing sister and that, 'I now belonged to her'. I could not have been more pleased – she was a 'cracker'. I was placed with the injured from Airborne and the other three with whom I had travelled were put with men from their units. When we were in the courtyard, waiting to be taken inside, a big cheer went up as a sergeant was brought in. He was from the same unit as some of the men around me and had been shot in his bottom – for the third time! To explain: infantrymen clearing wooded areas were often ambushed. They were allowed to pass a particular point and then shot at from the rear. This had been the case with this sergeant.

We were quickly settled into wards with doctors all over, checking this and that. I disliked the way they examined me and then looked at each other. The sister told me not to worry – I was going to be OK. Two sisters gave me a haircut, shave and a bed bath. I was well treated and enjoyed the experience. The feeling in my limbs was still absent but massage treatment helped to a certain extent. Three days I stayed at this place and was very sad to leave all those wonderful nursing staff. Everyone got on extremely well and there was a happy atmosphere. There were many tearful good-byes as we set off to join a hospital train destined for De-Haan, which is near the port of Ostende.

We were carried onto the train on our stretchers and placed on bunks along the sides of the carriages. This arrangement meant we had a better view than was the case when we were travelling in the ambulance. Some of the men on board were badly injured but there was no moaning or groaning from anyone throughout the journey. I must admit that I was very worried over not being able to feel anything in my right arm or leg.

The train stopped only a short distance from the hospital – named the 12th British General – to which we travelled by ambulance. This hospital had only just been opened and we were its first patients. The doctors carried out examinations the following morning and spent a long time discussing the bruising on the right side of my body. By this time, I was able to move slightly better and could see that my right side was black and blue. I must have landed with a heavy bump after being thrown in the air by the blast. The doctor said there would be a lot of pain when the feeling came back and that I would need to be sedated. He was correct in his prognosis; when the feeling started to return it was one big ache from my head to my toes. When I first managed to move my little finger it resulted in the worst stomach cramp I have ever experienced. I was moved to a room opposite the sister's office; sandbags were placed under my feet to stop me sliding down the bed and I was made to sit upright. It was not the most comfortable of positions.

Gradually, I began to feel better. The injections seemed to be working and the bruising was turning to a lighter shade of blue. My recovery continued and I was allowed to get up for one hour three times a day – morning, afternoon and again in the evening. As the pain subsided, I became more like my old self and did not need help with washing, shaving, cleaning teeth and going to the toilet; for this I thanked the Lord. I was also able to use the dining hall.

At the beginning of May 1945, I was transferred to a con- valescent home in a nearby village. I was a very happy person. On the first day I had several beers in the evening, met some new faces and felt at peace with the world. For the next seven days I spent the mornings running, the afternoons riding a bicycle and in the evenings I enjoyed a few beers. 8 May arrived and the end of the war in Europe; it was my mother's birthday.

The next day I was taken to Brugge where I stayed for two days. In Brugge, the Catholics staged processions to mark the end of the war and most interesting they were as I watched from my billet on the main street. It was then onto a train to Ostende to catch a boat to England. No matter how many times you left England and returned, it was always a great feeling to be back home. We docked at Dover, caught the train to London and shortly afterwards I was on my way home to Sheffield. I arrived home reasonably early. My Mum and Dad were still up. I did my usual act of walking in and grinning like a Cheshire cat. Something was wrong. Both my mother and sister, Joyce, were crying. My father looked as if he had seen a ghost. I went round asking what was the matter. Joyce then handed me a telegram from the War Office. It had a black border and said I was missing and believed to have been killed. Condolences were included.

Clearly the family were very upset and shocked, but pleased that I had returned. During the rest of my ten days' leave I watched them carefully as they were clearly distressed. I had asked someone to write to my parents explaining my situation and that I would not be writing home for a while; somehow the letter must have gone astray. It was good to see again my old mates in the local who teased me about, 'being always on leave'. I replied to the effect that someone had to see the local girls were all right with so many Yanks around.

My leave ended and I was unsure whether to return to the barracks at Bulford or go back to Europe and find my unit. Since I did not fancy the drilling in Bulford under some stranger, my decision was to find my unit wherever it might be located. Overnight I stayed in London and met up with some Yankee paras who had been with us in Holland; we had a good time. At the Union Jack Club, I got an early call and after breakfast caught a taxi to the station. The taxi driver refused my offer of payment. On the train to Dover, I gave some thought to how to get onto a boat without paperwork. Whether to be cheeky and just march on board regardless, or to report to the RTO was considered at some length. I decided not to bother the RTO – it was too risky and I was never very good at fastening up all of my buttons. At the quayside, I made myself look busy with some rolled-up papers and looked around for a boat about to sail. A group of young fellows was boarding one of the vessels and I asked where they were going. They told me their orders were to fetch some Latvians and Estonians, who had been working for the Germans, back to the UK. My unit was in France and so I decided to join them. We arrived in Calais the following morning. No one had asked me any questions.

I disembarked and walked along the quayside and pondered what to do next. Then I looked at the boat docked next to the one I had just left. Some faces seemed familiar. Looking more closely it dawned on me that it was my unit – the 5th Parachute Brigade – which was embarking. Grinning from ear to ear, I walked up the gangplank and everyone and everything stopped. 'We thought you were dead,' was the phrase on nearly everybody's lips; they were all shocked when they saw me. I gave my officer an account of what had happened and he said, 'I never thought I would see you again – it's unbelievable'. He added that they would have to get used to putting up with me again. I had returned!

It was good to be back with my mates. One or two said it had been quiet without me. I looked forward to starting another bridge school and boozing again in Andover. With a great deal of pleasure I accepted an invitation to be best man to one of the lads at his wedding in Salisbury. Flying swastika flags, obtained as souvenirs, we returned in convoy to Bulford; no one was left in any doubt that the 6th Airborne was back home. It was a lovely feeling.

At Bulford, the brigadier gave us a talk and, after many congratulations, told us the 5th Parachute Brigade was to be posted overseas to the South East Asia Command. First stop was to be India. An advance party was to be sent by air and the rest by ship. His good news was that before all this happened, everyone would have a leave of ten days.

My Mum and Dad did not know what to say when they were told I would soon be on my way to India. There was no 'WELCOME HOME FRED' stuff for me. My unit still had men who could fight and they were needed on the other side of the world. Leave did not seem at all the same now the European war had ended. It had been arranged that I would meet up with my mates in London towards the end of our leave. So off I went for what turned out to be one great binge after which it was time to return to our unit. We arrived at Waterloo station not really caring whether or not we caught the train; time was not one of our strong points – particularly when returning from leave. It is a different matter altogether when on duty. The next day we were told in no uncertain manner to pull our socks up, draw our kit from the stores and get ready for jungle warfare. We had made a name for ourselves in Europe and now we were expected to do so in the Far East.

16

South East Asia – India

The clothing we were issued with was dark green and known as 'Jungle Greens'. Each man was also provided with a *Panga* knife for cutting through the undergrowth in the jungle, new boots for the expected wet weather and a *Poncho* cape which was waterproof. Other items included a mess tin, knife, fork, spoon and a mirror; all these were made of stainless steel. The mirror was something of a luxury as when I was in the desert it was a matter of shaving from memory. Because we had to live rough did not mean we had to look untidy. After checking our equipment we paraded in the medical inspection room for our injections. Four were required which was more than I had ever been given at the same time. Two doctors faced another two doctors and as each of us passed between the first pair an injection was given in each arm. We then moved forward to the second pair for a further jab in both arms. To avoid very sore and painful arms, we were told that it was necessary to move the fluid around the body as quickly as possible. We went back to our barrack room and set about polishing the floor with a Bumper which we took in turns. It worked and the floor looked very shiny when we had finished. A period of 48 hours was granted to get over the injections but we were not allowed to go out of the barracks. Instead we slept and played cards.

One of the lads got a severe bout of earache but whether this was anything to do with the jabs I do not know. We gave him an injection of morphine that helped to ease the pain. All Paras were issued with five ampoules of morphine for personal use in case they were needed in action. If you were injured and nothing else was available they could be extremely useful for relieving pain. They were also handy for earache.

Some of us were told that we would be flying out to India in an advance party. The rest were to go by sea. Everyone wanted to fly and so the news caused a bit of unrest for a time. When a few of the lads learned we would be flying from Brize Norton they were delighted; they knew some WAAFs who were stationed there and thought they would be well away. They were in for a disappointment as it was a case of straight on to a Dakota aircraft as soon as we arrived at the airfield. We were introduced to the three members of the crew who were to fly us to India. There were two pilots and a wireless operator. With our gear safely aboard the aircraft prepared for takeoff. It was the usual cloudy weather in England but we were quickly above the clouds and into a marvellously clear sky.

The crew told us that it would take five days to reach Karachi in India providing we did not run into any problems. Our first stop was Sardinia which we reached on the evening of the first day. A 4 o'clock takeoff was scheduled for the next morning and, after a good meal, we immediately went off for a few hours' sleep. It was still dark and the lights on the airfield shone brilliantly when we made our way to the aircraft the next morning. The runway was relatively short and went right up to the water's edge. We had been warned not to go near the toilet during takeoff as it made the pilot's job more difficult. Anxiously, we watched as we accelerated for takeoff, and shortly before reaching the sea, we felt the plane rising. We had avoided a soaking and we gave the pilot a big cheer.

When we were in the air again, the pilot let us know that we were heading for El Adem in Libya. For me, this was ground I had covered with the 51st Highland Division and to which I had not expected ever to return. After being given this information, most of us fell asleep; this is something we could do very easily when there was not much else to do. Some time later I woke up and strolled up to the crew's cabin. They also were having a good sleep. The pilot stirred and said, 'I did enjoy that sleep. Thank the Lord for George, we could not manage without him.' 'George', the automatic pilot was definitely a wonderful invention.

The coast of Libya came into sight and I saw the salt flats where we had raced with our jeeps. Libya was seen from a different perspective. It was fascinating seeing North Africa laid out before me. I thought flying classrooms would be an excellent method of teaching Geography. It was much more pleasant flying above it than travelling on its surface. As we continued, I saw Tripoli, Tobruk and over to the Egyptian border. When we got near to Tobruk, the Trigh-Capuzzo track came into view.

We came into El Adem from the sea and how different it was compared with November 1942. We had a first-class meal that was much better than the bully stew I had on my previous visit. We stayed only a short while before setting off again for the short trip to Lydda in Palestine where we landed in the evening. The sleeping quarters were on the airfield and comprised underground chambers with tented roofs. They were warm and clean with bunks down each side. The food provided could not be faulted. Again it was an early start the following morning for the next stage of our journey which was to Iraq.

As we flew further eastwards, the weather took a turn for the worse. Fierce winds battered the Dakota and it was difficult to make out the desert below with the storm that was raging. The plane was leaking oil from the starboard engine but it continued to perform. Iraq is noted for very windy weather and dust storms. One of the pilots said it was usual both to land there and take off again in storm conditions. There was nothing we could do to help, so we went back to sleep until it was time to land. The airport at which we landed was, I believe, called Shaiba. That is how it sounded anyway. The wind was gale force and there was grit absolutely everywhere. I have a relative who was stationed in Iraq for three years. That he does not talk about it is understandable; it is enough to send anybody crazy. My father was also here during the First World War and he had to break the ice in the winter mornings to get water for washing. Thank the Lord my stay was only overnight. There was not much going for this place but the food was good and the sleeping quarters were very clean and serviceable. A strong gale was still blowing as we took to the air the next morning and you could hear grit bouncing on the fuselage of the plane. Our next port-of-call was an airfield in the Persian Gulf which also had its problems. Here the sun tried to shine through a permanent haze that was ever present. The men and women stationed here did not have a sun tan as might have been expected; they looked more yellow than brown. We took the opportunity to use the swimming pool during the two hours required to carry out the refuelling. The sticky heat was really oppressive and the water in the pool was lovely and cool. When the plane was ready for takeoff, the pilot revved the engines to let us know we had to return for the next leg of our journey to Karachi in India.

In the plane there were flies everywhere as we took off. We had bets on which would be the first to fall asleep – as they all did when the plane reached about 2,000 feet. When they had all dropped off, they were swept up in a heap and put down the toilet. The pilot then informed us that we would soon be flying over the Indian Ocean and that monsoon weather was expected. Our type seldom worried about such trivial matters as wind or rain and we all settled down to either a game of cards or another period of 'shuteye'. What a shock we got a short time later. The wind hit us with a force that was staggering. Dakotas are good planes and this one was no exception. It ploughed on but went down from its usual height of 12,000 feet to about 2,000. The pilot informed us that if we continued to lose height it would be necessary to jettison the door. We were accustomed to flying without a door when we were parachuting and so we were not unduly concerned. When the order to release the door came we acted very quickly and it was gone inside a couple of seconds or so. I estimated we were then flying at about 400 feet and we could actually see sharks down below waiting for us. Then came the cry, 'Dinghy, dinghy'. This was a drill for reducing casualties should it be necessary to ditch the aircraft. We all got in a line and sat down with our backs to the bulkhead next to the pilot's cabin. Other men sat close up between our open legs. As we sat there we considered how we could get on top of the plane when it was ditched – hoping that it would stay afloat.

The pilot continued to wrestle with the controls and he managed to keep the Dakota in the air. After what seemed to be eternity, the plane rose to about 1,000 feet and the pilot announced we were going to be all right. When we had climbed to about 2,000 feet he allowed us to return to our seats. The sharks had to find something else for their next meal.

We were informed that the monsoon had eased and that we were making our way up the northwest frontier of India. The airfield at which we landed was about two miles inland. As we came in to land we could see a huge chasm at the end of the runway. Afterwards, we were taken to this part of the airfield by some RAF chaps stationed there; two transport planes lay wrecked at the bottom. They had tried to take off but were too heavily loaded and had paid the price.

The RAF men did not get many visitors here but they had heard about us and made us very welcome. On the next day they showed us the way to the sea. As we went through the airfield gates there was a rough dirt track that passed near a village. On this road we saw several control towers standing about 30 feet high, each guarded by seven or eight men. They were *Pathan* tribesmen who carried long rifles and, we were told, would use them if necessary. They eyed us up and down as though we had no right to be there; it was slightly unnerving. As we passed near the village we saw many of the huts were made out of square four-gallon petrol cans that were used by the forces. The cans were filled with sand and formed the walls of the huts. It must have been very hot inside.

The sea was nice. We did not have costumes – that was something the army did not issue. Most of the afternoon was spent crabbing; there were countless hermit crabs around. In the evening we went to an open-air theatre on the airfield for a cowboy and Indian show. Later we were invited to a drinking party where there was beer and food, but no women were permitted to attend.

The name of the airfield was Juarni. The next morning we took off once again, this time for Karachi. As we travelled down the runway there were a few jokes about the chasm. We missed it easily and once in the air we went through the usual procedure of sweeping up the horde of flies and getting rid of them. No one went near the toilet when preparing to land as the flies would wake up and be feeling more than a little hungry.

The land was generally brown and bare as we flew towards Karachi. It was mainly agricultural with very few buildings. In sight of Karachi there were many ships in the harbour; it is a big port and was busy. When we had landed it was time for another of those agonising good-byes. We had got to know the crew of the Dakota extremely well – particularly over the Indian Ocean. They were all great guys and we were sorry we would not be seeing them again. The first pilot was due to get married on his return to Brize Norton and so we emptied our pockets of all of our English money and gave it to him to buy a present for his new wife. All together it would have made for a decent gift.

As we disembarked, several Indian men descended upon us and offered to carry our bags. It was explained that this was the custom in India. For a few *ackers* you could have a shave, a manicure, your toenails cut or even corns removed, if you had any. Our first call was at the restaurant which was very well run and where we had a first-class meal. We were then taken to tented accommodation situated close to the airfield. The beds were called *Charpoys*. They were made of wood and had low-slung ropes on which was placed a straw mattress. We found them really comfortable and slept like logs.

The following morning, I woke up suddenly to find an Indian man standing in front of me with a cut-throat razor in his hand. He was laughing. I felt my face and found he had already shaved one side. This had been done while I was fast asleep. I allowed him to finish but told him not to attempt to do it ever again. There was no telling what bits I might find missing. Another chap then brought me tea and cakes which I had in bed. This was a custom to which I could easily have become accustomed, as it were. You had to pay, of course, but it was not much and it was enjoyable.

A day or so later we moved into barracks in Karachi. Since leaving Brize Norton we had travelled first class; we now returned to normal. Over the next few days we got an idea of India and its people. A tour round the docks was arranged and I watched one of our chaps have a corn removed. An old Indian placed a small shell over the corn and sucked hard for ten or fifteen minutes; it came out as clean as a whistle. We found it an altogether different way of life.

It had been arranged for our unit to travel to Bombay, a four- to five-day journey. A train had been laid on for us and we boarded it early one morning. It was very hot and when we had cleared the city, I changed into my pyjamas and sat on the steps of the carriage. I wore them most of the way to Bombay but no one seemed to mind. Initially we made our way through mountainous country where the scenery was really impressive. On that first day I stayed on the carriage steps until it was dark and then went inside. The train did not have glass in the windows. In its place were wooden screens that folded up and down; they made a noise but let in plenty of air. We all slept on wooden seats but no one complained.

The next day the scenery changed to that of a desert. It went on for many miles, just scrub and sand – much like the western desert of North Africa. Later that day, we passed near a large city, not unlike an Arab city I had seen in Libya. This one was much larger with a number of tall buildings built in red sandstone. Mosques with their minarets dominated the horizon. It was a very interesting part of India. We stopped at a small halt to take water on board. Orders had been given that no one was to attempt to get off the train as the natives were not too friendly towards us. Apparently, it was some sort of private kingdom inside a walled city and which had its own king. Camels seemed to be a popular form of transport judging by the number of them moving around. It was also interesting to see the people going down to the river where they washed their clothes. Usually, when a train stopped in a station, many youngsters would come clamouring for 'Baksheesh'. Here they kept themselves strictly to themselves. I tried to find out the name of the place but drew a complete blank. The train crew did not understand what I was saying; that is what they said anyway. Two hours later we were on our way again. I resumed my seat on the steps of the carriage. No company was needed – I was content just to gaze across the deserted landscape. That afternoon I saw several groups of people on camels making their way, no doubt, to that city for which I could not find a name. They did not wave and neither did I.

When it was dark it was usually a time for sleeping; this particular evening was an exception. We had been asleep for only a short while when we were woken by a loud banging and rattling. The train had run into a big cloud of flying locusts. They were everywhere, between five and six inches long, and they came in through every opening they could find. We set about killing them but there were so many it hardly made any difference. Some men would do the killing while others filled buckets and threw them outside. There was no more rest that night and we were still at it the following day into the afternoon. The only locusts I had previously seen were in North Africa; they were about two inches long and still in the walking stage. These were something entirely different.

By this time, our carriage was in a terrible mess and cleaning it up was our next priority. When we thought we had finished we found more dead bodies. I eventually returned to my place on the carriage steps and wondered what would happen next. The countryside gradually changed from plain desert to small areas of greenery and the odd palm tree. People started appearing, and also water buffalo pulling carts or walking in circles drawing water from a well. These beasts were massive and I saw one knock a 5cwt truck over on its side. India may have been the jewel of the crown of the British Empire, and from what I saw of it, I would say it was a many-sided jewel. I witnessed both the spectacular sights and the downright poverty of some of its inhabitants. It was an experience that I shall always remember.

We made good progress. With only two days to go before reaching our destination, I was obliged to get back into uniform. We were nearing a built-up area and needed to present a reasonable appearance. I continued with my studying of the countryside and the inhabitants from my outside seat. The train moved slowly through some parts of the city and I was able clearly to see crowds of people milling around. Their police were also in attendance in sizeable numbers, all carrying a long brown cane called a 'lahti', which they seemed to use on the public quite often for no reason that was immediately apparent.

On what we thought would be the next-to-last day of our journey to Bombay, we were informed of an alteration to our schedule. Instead of going into Bombay, we went straight into a camp at a place called Kalyann where we arrived that evening. Kalyann was a brown, dusty place on a hillside. We were taken from the station in trucks to No. 4 camp. Settling in took the usual form, with everyone wanting their little space but there were no major problems. A river ran through the camp and the locals told us the hill on which the camp had been built was called Cobra Hill. There were holes along the river bank where cobras lived during the day, usually coming out at night. There was a big NAAFI that was well stocked with drink and sold what they called *Tomato Banjos*. They were big bread cakes filled with tomatoes – quite filling but not exactly to our liking.

On our first morning at this camp we went along to the cookhouse for breakfast. We carried it on a plate out of the building and in less than a second it was all gone. Great big birds swooped down and the breakfast vanished. The locals were laughing and it seemed all newcomers were caught out in this way. These birds were known as Kite Hawks, but we had our own name for the blighters that was not entirely dissimilar. I made sure I never lost my breakfast to them again. As for the cobras, we did see several in a morning when they had been hit on the head with a spade or something.

I was given the task of taking some messages to HQ in Bombay. I was told to look my best. No problem, I said. About 7 a.m., I set off in an open-top jeep. I had forgotten about the monsoons; three times I got soaked and dried out before reaching Bombay. With each soaking, I became more dishevelled and felt dreadful when I handed over the documents, particularly as everybody at HQ looked as if they just come out of a Burton's shop window.

An NCO had asked me to deliver a letter to an Indian girl who lived in the YWCA in Bombay. I found the building easily enough but finding the girl was more of a problem. The YWCA had a large number of rooms and I was passed from one girl to another – all extremely attractive. Eventually, I found the right one and she was pleased to see me. After handing over the letter I had a meal and set about exploring the city.

There were the usual cows in the streets and no one seemed to care where they went or what they did. Cows are, I believe, considered to be sacred animals throughout India. I went into a little corner shop and a cow followed me inside. The shop-keeper smiled, shrugged his shoulders and saw to the cow before serving me. I imagined this sort of thing happening in Tottenham Court Road. Opposite this shop was a large grey concrete tower with a domed top. I was intrigued and asked the shop-keeper, who spoke good English, for details. He answered me very quietly and said it was a 'tower of silence' where Indians of a certain caste were taken and left when they had died. I could not get any more information from him or anyone else. Coming out of Bombay, into the more rural areas, I saw some piles of wood built up as bonfires at the sides of the road. These were for cremating the dead, and a few days later, I witnessed from a distance a cremation being carried out. It was interesting to see how seriously those in charge took their responsibilities. An older man went around the fire continually probing and checking the condition of the cremation.

Men in my old regiment, the Essex, had told me that disease was rife when they had served out in India. They were given inoculations in the groin with a very large needle and the pain was something awful. I was very pleased that there had been a big improvement in conditions in India since their time, but I was very wary about the packs of dogs found in the villages for fear of catching rabies.

Nearly every day there was something new or different. I saw a youngster sitting at the side of a goat with an udder in his mouth. On one occasion, I watched young children being read stories by a man who went round several villages. It was well worth watching to see the expressions on the children's faces. They showed everything – fear, surprise, concern, horror and laughter as the stories were told. These children did not have books, pens or pencils and there was no radio. Their education was limited to these visits on one day a week. I waited until the lesson was over before speaking to the man. He spoke good English and was pleased that I had shown an interest in the children's welfare.

On another day I came across a commotion in a village and went to investigate. The people were running all over and diving for cover, some jumping into a nearby lake. Everybody was very frightened and understandably so. I was told a hornet's nest had been disturbed and, believe me, that was asking for trouble. The hornets in India are very big and they attack on sight without mercy. To be stung by a hornet was serious and hospital treatment lasting a least a month was usually necessary. They have been known to sting so savagely that the person concerned has died as a result. The people who had jumped into the water were given a hard time as the hornets hovered over them. Those who came out were immediately stung. This went on for quite a long time and then, suddenly, the hornets gave up their attack and left in a swarm. I helped with the treatment of some of those who had been stung. A man produced a concoction which we pasted onto the areas which had been affected and it seemed to ease the pain a little. What the paste contained and how effective it was I do not know. I continued to learn a little bit about India; keep away from this, do not do that and whatever you do do, be very careful.

14 August 1945 arrived – the day that Japan surrendered. There was to be no more fighting in Malaya and it appeared we had come all this way for nothing. The next day there was a big parade of the Airborne Forces. I was on duty that day

and so did not attend but, of course, was later told what had happened.

Our brigade had made a good name for itself in Europe and was justly proud of its considerable achievements. We were prepared for most things but not for the surprise we received. The parade was told in no uncertain terms that wartime soldiers were no longer required; what the brigade needed now was parade-ground soldiers. The officer who said this caused a great deal of bad feeling in the ranks. We were shattered and everyone proceeded to get very drunk. The next day, the atmosphere was tense. A few careless words had caused a lot of damage to morale. In the evening we again drowned our sorrows with a drinking session. Around 10 o'clock I decided to answer the call of nature. I sat on the toilet seat and made myself comfortable. Suddenly, I felt something touch my bottom. In a flash I was gone. The man who said that a woman could run faster with her skirts up than a man could with trousers round his ankles did not know what he was talking about. I was back in the canteen, with my trousers round my ankles in double-quick time. My father, who had served in the army in India, had told me never to go to the toilet after dark as this was the time snakes would go in to feed. I had laughed at the time but was not laughing on this occasion. If your bottom was bitten by a snake, the application of a tourniquet was out of the question. My encounter with the snake was good for a laugh among the lads but I never ever again used the toilets at night while I was in India, or anywhere else in southeast Asia for that matter.

I was involved in an accident one afternoon when riding a motorcycle on the main road that ran through the camps. A 3-ton truck in front of me turned to the right without giving a signal at the same time as I was about to overtake. The bike ended in a ditch and I slid under the back axle of the truck with the offside rear wheel running over me. Everything went black and I could neither see nor breathe. I jumped up with the idea of forcing air into my lungs. It worked and my vision returned. There was a Red Cross hut nearby and I made my way to it somehow or other. The medics placed me on a stretcher and told me I had some ribs which were broken. I was taken to the hospital in Kalyann.

The hospital was staffed by RAMC men from one of our battalions – most likely the 7th Parachute. I could not thank them enough for their attention to my injuries. When I was first admitted, I was examined by a doctor who tried to inject me from the back. We had one hell of a row. I told him, without mincing my words, that I did not want any morphine at that time and would give it to myself should the need arise. The doctor got a rollicking from the man in overall charge.

I was placed on a bed in a room with other dodgy cases. An arrangement of sandbags and a metal frame supported my body. Any movement was difficult with five ribs broken inwardly and also crushed stomach muscles. The next day I had several visitors who all wanted to see the man who had been run over by a truck and had got up and run a hundred yards for help. That was me! I just lay there and smiled. Actually there was little else I could do at the time – my back was raw from sliding on the gravel and if I moved a finger too quickly the result would be a cramp in my stomach.

In those days the treatment for broken ribs was to wrap elasticated bandages around the body. These were changed once a week and their removal was horrendous. The hair underneath grew for seven days and got caught up in the bandage material. If you tried to remove them yourself you did it very slowly. Matron had no trouble – she just ripped them off, and I mean ripped. At least it was over reasonably quickly.

After two weeks in the small ward opposite the nurses' station, I was transferred to the main ward. As my recovery progressed, I was allowed out of bed for a period in the afternoons. This was a great relief since I was fed up of being in bed, having bed baths and not being able to go to the toilet. I got much pleasure out of doing things for myself.

One morning we had a visit from two Labour Members of Parliament. They went round asking how we felt about the election of a Labour government. Politics are of no interest to me and, since I did not wish to listen to their claptrap, I asked for a bedpan and they quickly moved to the far end of the ward.

Cobras would occasionally manage to get into the wards and everybody would quickly get out of their way. The hospital employed Indian men as sweepers and it was one of their jobs to get the snakes outside and dispose of them. The sweepers would remove them from the wards by beating a brush on the floor and they did not seem to be concerned about being bitten as we were. I found the cobras fascinating to watch but never ventured too close.

When I had been in hospital for about a month, there was an accident at the railway station in Kalyann where we had arrived. A soldier had been run over by a train and had lost his foot. He was in a bad way. A nursing sister asked for volunteers to sit with him and keep him company. I was feeling much better and offered my services along with a chap from the Royal Engineers. We took turns to be by his side. Most of the time he was shouting for his father who was in Ireland. We did not get much opportunity to talk as he was raving incoherently for long periods. Two days after he was admitted we noticed a strong smell of violets and on the third day he died. It was not a pleasant duty but I hope we helped in some small way.

My recovery continued and I could not find enough to occupy my time. I was, therefore, delighted when a message came through to the ward from 'theatre' asking if, 'that Para bloke would like to help in theatre?' Of course, I jumped at the opportunity of being able to do something useful and was the first to arrive at the theatre the following Monday morning. After being introduced to all the staff, we then prepared for the operation. I was detailed to help the anaesthetist who turned out to be the doctor with whom I had had an argument when first admitted. He did not turn me down as I expected – he just smiled and asked me to get some swabs from the cupboard. Ether was then used for anaesthetizing patients which was a slow and tedious business. The surgeon would explain what he was doing and I learned a lot. After each operation, the theatre staff would go into another room for a rest, the surgeon would get out his whisky bottle and give us all a tot. By the end of the day we were all feeling great.

I would have liked a regular job in that hospital but the day came when I was considered fit enough to be sent on a month's convalescence. The powers that be sent me to a camp on the coast a few miles above Bombay which was called *The Star Studded Beaches of Ju-Jhu*. It was an army camp that had a NAAFI which sold those never-to-be-forgotten *Tomato Banjos*. Together with three other chaps, I lived in an Indian *basha* hut which was only a matter of a hundred yards from the seashore; the sand was lovely and we did a lot of sunbathing. Once a week we would take a truck into Bombay and visit the cinema or go for a drink. It was all unbelievable.

At the end of the month I was as fit as I had ever been. Our brigade had already set off for Malaya and, with other Airborne men, I was sent by train from Bombay to join them in Calcutta. It was a very long journey taking us right across the breadth of India. Also on the train were the rear parties of our three battalions and all together it was a very large detachment that was on board. It was not possible to sit in pyjamas on the steps of the railway carriage on this journey. There was nothing lax about discipline this time.

One day we pulled into a small station way out in the country. A group of Indian men was deep in conversation on the platform. I called out and asked for the name of the station. The person who answered me was the teacher who went round the villages reading stories to children. I got off the train and had a good chat with him, telling of my argument with a truck and my time in hospital. He also had not been very well, having picked up something in one of the villages. I had to pay my respects to him and his family very quickly as the train set off again without any warning. He said we would meet again but, I regret to say, so far we have not done so and the chances of now doing so are slim.

At times it was very hot and sticky on the train and we were very pleased when it arrived in Calcutta on the day it was scheduled to do so – an unusual event in India at that particular time. We were taken to a tented camp on the local airfield where we stayed for a couple of days before joining a ship to which was take us to Singapore. The two days were spent on trips into Calcutta for shopping, drinking or whatever – you name it, it was available. Troops of all nations would be in the clubs at night and there were frequent fights. The Charinghi Road in Calcutta was a place that resembled parts of Cairo and whether you went there was entirely up to you. We finished one evening with a race between a group of Aussies and ourselves, up and down Charinghi Road in Indian horse-drawn carriages called *gharries*. I do not remember who won, only that we had a lot of fun

Our break ended and we assembled at the docks to join an Indian ship with the name *SS Agra*. From the outside it looked like a 'rust-bucket' to say the very least. As the men crowded onto the messdecks they found cockroaches everywhere and some very big ones too. We chased several rats from spaces intended for storing our gear. It was an absolute disgrace and so we all walked off the ship, back on to the quay. Our officers tried to reason with us, but to no avail. The ship's officers and ours went into a huddle. We could not stay on the docks, we had to meet up with our brigade in Malaya and no other ship was available. It was decided we would all sleep on deck and no one would go below for any reason – not even to eat. The washing facilities were situated on the upper deck, so this did not present a problem. We rigged up tents and bivouacs on the deck in order to keep out of the sun. Never before had I seen a ship so festooned with so much canvas on its deck. And so we left India having made the best out of a decidedly bad job.

17

South East Asia – Singapore & Java

Some of the men had pets, such as parrots and monkeys, and they had spent a great deal of time discussing how they were to get them on board. It was not permitted to take animals on to a ship and the Captain could, if he so wished, dispose of them overboard. This threat had been known to have been carried out previously and, consequently, it was very risky to attempt to smuggle pets on board. When going onto the ship, I noticed that some of the men were carrying their large packs on their backs. It was usual to carry the small pack on our backs and to place the large pack in our kitbag. We later discovered that the animals had been given a shot of morphine which knocked them out for about 24 hours.

I travelled at the aft end of the ship which was rather noisy due to the ship's screws. It was, probably, similar to travelling 'steerage class' to America at the turn of the century. A kitchen was set up on the aft well deck. I tried to stick to sausage, rice, beans and the odd chicken. Our officers ate up forward with the ship's officers and I hope they enjoyed the cabbages that were on the menu. We had sight of these vegetables being collected by the cooks from under a tarpaulin on the deck. When the sheet was removed there were so many cockroaches the cabbages could not be seen. The native cooks were unconcerned and everything went down to the kitchen. They probably regarded it as good protein. I gave it a miss.

The pets which had been brought aboard began to come

round somewhere in the middle of the Indian Ocean. I noticed the crew were not very pleased to have them on board but the Captain did not say anything at all. He could not be regarded as a disciplinarian and was never seen making a tour of inspection around the ship.

The ship travelled, flat out, at eight knots and we came in sight of Singapore early one morning just before October 1945. A member of the crew pointed out the tallest structure – the Cathay building. It was a cinema with a large restaurant at the top. The harbour was busy with a large number of Chinese unloading ships by hand in what appeared to be a disorganised manner, and which took a great deal of time.

We filed ashore and gathered into our separate units. It was not long before those of us from HQ were collected and taken to join our colleagues at a base which occupied a whole street of new houses. We were pleased to see our mates again. My first job, the following day, was to join a squad of men in charge of Japanese prisoners of war. Our group was under the control of a Corporal Revill – a massive man who I had at last decided could not be beaten in a fair fight. All he had to do was to lie on me and any movement was out of the question. He weighed around eighteen stones against my eleven and a half. Apart from that we were good pals. The Japanese POWs were taken each day to the docks for the purpose of loading and unloading ships which was done mainly by hand. They were very good workers – short in stature but strong and willing to work. The ships they worked on were quickly turned round. In the Japanese army, there was no such thing as a sick parade. If they were ill they went on parade regardless – even with malaria – and were only allowed to see a doctor if they were considered ill enough not to be wasting his time. Later, we had several Japanese doctors attached to our unit and they proved to be very able, curing such things as ringworm that some men had, probably, caught from their pet monkeys. Their doctors were also good at handling ulcers with which our medics seemed to have problems.

Dealing with the POWs was strange; they insisted on bowing to you whenever you went anywhere near them. I once got out of my jeep when near a field in which there were several hundred prisoners and they all stood to attention and bowed to me.

Chinese teams also worked on the docks, unloading and loading ships. They were paid for each round trip in which they carried something off the ship down one gangplank and brought something else on up the other. After they had done a few of these trips and been paid, they would disappear among the crates that were stored on the quayside and become involved in a game of *Mahjong* or another Chinese pastime. They were inveterate gamblers. If they won they continued to play and if they lost they would join the queue and start work again. It was their way of life which no one seemed capable of changing.

The British had imposed a curfew on Singapore in the evenings and the city was patrolled to make sure there were no violations of the order. When our turn came for this duty, we set off intending to be very strict and to stand no nonsense from anyone. We cruised around the shopping area as quietly as possible but did not see anyone about or anything suspicious. It was then decided we would take a look at the docks. The Chinese were not averse to a little pilfering – not much different to any other nationality – and we thought we might catch one or two in the act. Away we went down the maze of narrow streets and lanes that comprised the docks. Whenever it was possible, we would cut the engine and glide down a slope very quietly. This ruse paid off and we caught a party gambling on a street corner. For them it was a case of grab what they could and scarper. They would leave food, cards, cigarettes, pipes and also money. There was usually a crowd of them – always

Chinese, never Malayans for some reason. We would upset four or five gangs a night in this way but they would return to exactly the same spot the following evening.

We returned to the docks one night and upset the usual gangs trying to steal some goods stacked on the quayside. One group we came across had a large black car that was being stacked with tobacco as we arrived. On seeing us they dived into the car and were off. We had seen them before but each time they had made good their escape. This time we tried different tactics and after a chase we managed to block them off – they had no means of escaping. We went to pick them up but the driver of the black car put his foot down and drove it over the edge of the quay into the water. Looking down into the dock was like trying to see down a coal mine. It was very dark and as the quay was suspended on piles it was impossible to see underneath. The car had gone under and although we kept very quiet we did not hear a sound. What had happened to the men we did not know at the time. The police had been alerted and they continued with the search as we went on to patrol elsewhere.

After finishing duty that evening, I was having a drink and a game of cards in a billet with some friends. About midnight an NCO came through the door. He was soaking wet and there had been no rain that evening. A big laugh went up and there was a lot of joking as to how he had got into such a state. My friends did not know I had been at the docks earlier that evening and I did not enlighten them. The NCO then proceeded to tell us that he had been driving a car which had gone over the dockside and into the water. All the passengers had managed to get out before the car had sunk and the NCO had led the party back to dry land – involving a swim of two or three miles. I did not say anything – not a word. To do so might have had unpleasant consequences and I am not noted for being a long-distance swimmer!

I got to know Singapore extremely well and really enjoyed my time in the big leisure centres such as the *Old World* and other similar places. The Airborne had taken over the boxing and wrestling halls and provided most of the champions. I had a white suit made and became accustomed to travelling around Singapore in a rickshaw. The chap who pulled it used to pick me up at my billet which was very good for my ego.

Another place I visited was the Toc H also in Singapore. There they served some good meals and I got to know a young Chinese girl who was a waitress in the canteen. She told me that she had taken the job as a means of improving her English. When the Chinese set out to do something they would do so with total commitment and I met several who had their own businesses. We got on very well and I asked her to go to the Cathay cinema one evening. She agreed and it was arranged we would meet the next evening at a point opposite the cinema. The chap who pulled my rickshaw picked me up in ample time in order not to be late. He was all smiles as usual and everything seemed to be in order. When he arrived near the cinema I offered him the fare as usual but he said there was nothing to pay. I said to him that it was his living and he could not afford do it for free, but he was adamant that he would not take any payment and went on his way. This was the first time I had come across a rickshaw man refusing to take the fare and I suspected something was amiss. I walked to the point were we had arranged to meet and noted there were a number of Chinese men and women standing around as if they were gathering to go somewhere. Some elderly men came and stood near where I was standing. They smiled and, being polite, I smiled in return. Then I saw the girl I was taking to the cinema, coming towards me. She was accompanied by several other women but I still did not understand what was happening. I smiled and went forward to greet her and was immediately surrounded by a large crowd; it seemed they all intended to accompany us into the theatre. A quick calculation of my finances had convinced me that I could not afford to pay the admission charges for everyone. She sensed my nervousness and, squeezing my hand, said I was not to worry since everything had been taken care of, including the rickshaw man. This was the way things were done in Singapore among the Chinese, and she added that I would get used to the situation. I do not remember crossing the road or going up the cinema steps – I just went along with the crowd. If I had known what was going to happen it would not have happened. Anna, which was the pet name I had given her, was quite content and seemed to be enjoying the evening. I could not do a thing wrong. Everything I did was met with nods and smiles. Anna and I were so busy whispering to each other that we did not take much notice of the picture which was a favourite of the Chinese people called *Fu Man Chu.* They thought that the Westerner's idea of a Chinaman was great and there were many big laughs all round. Ice creams were passed to us up the aisle. Anna's father was very generous and had everything organised.

After the show we both went up to the roof restaurant surrounded by our bodyguard. It was lovely – in the open air, a pleasant evening and lots of good food. We were given pride of place overlooking the city lights. The waiters could not do enough for us. I told Anna she must be some sort of Princess, the way everybody bowed to her. She smiled and said that Daddy was a big businessman in Singapore. I was extremely concerned where it would all end. There was no way that I could possibly compete with her lifestyle. It would not have been fair that I should lead Anna on and I decided, there and then, to quietly fade out of her life.

We left the restaurant with everyone nodding and saying how they had enjoyed the whole evening. One big happy group, we arrived at the place we met and where the rickshaw man was waiting to take me back to Brigade HQ and reality. I said goodnight to Anna and she made me promise to come and see her again at the Toc H. For the first time in my life an evening out had not cost me a penny and it had been thoroughly enjoyable.

The following day I was detailed to accompany an officer to a meeting at Changhi Jail. This place had an awful reputation for cruelty to allied prisoners of war by the Japanese. When we arrived, there were Australians still there who were so ill they could not be moved. I saw one man who weighed a little over four stones. Others who were moving about were not much better and looked dreadful. Opposite Changhi Jail there were barracks where there was a U-boat captain from Kiel. What he was doing there I did not find out. He was the only German I saw out there. His U-boat was under guard by the British Navy.

From there we went on to visit one of our battalions which was stationed on the grounds of a race course at Bukit Timah. We had to make arrangements for a party of men to take over some islands near Singapore. While we had been in Singapore, our battalions had been busy clearing some of the islands but a few remained occupied, with the Japanese refusing to sur-render. It was not originally intended that I should be a member of one of the landing parties, so I volunteered to go as a driver and was accepted. Several groups set off at the same time for the various destinations. When we were on board our ship, we were told that our destination was a large island that had a strong garrison of Japanese troops.

When we arrived at our island the ship anchored about a mile offshore and the first party went ashore in small boats. They landed quietly and other parties followed at intervals, with our group forming the rearguard. Once ashore we set about the task of taking over some transport. I got hold of a 3-ton truck and was directed, with others, to go inland to pick up Japanese prisoners. Going through the rubber plantations we came to a group of buildings dominated by a large sprawling house. Our men were all over and they had dozens of Japanese soldiers together with their officers lined up outside awaiting our collection. The prisoners were bundled into the trucks and taken to the quay to be ferried to the waiting ship. I noticed that some were looking very surly but we stood no nonsense and packed them tightly into the ferry boat. As the boat set off, first one, then quite a few jumped into the water. The officer in charge of our men gave instructions to let them go if that was what they wanted. By the time the boat got about halfway to the mother ship the prisoners had stopped jumping from the boat. We then went off to pick up another load and when we returned the attempts to commit *hara-kiri* had ceased. Some who were still in the water were shouting to be picked up and were told they would have to wait until all the others were safely on board. Had a shark come along it would have been hard luck. Having completed our task we returned to Singapore and our billets.

The weather had moved into the showery season and the best thing was to remove all your clothes and dance around in the rain. This way you cooled off and felt very clean. Some of the lads had prickly heat, but I was one of the lucky ones. While I was there I picked up a little stray dog that I trained. We all slept on the floor and every morning socks and shoes would be missing. Whether I or the dog became the best known is a matter of conjecture.

I had promised to visit Anna at the Toc H and we all know how easy it is to find an excuse for not doing something we ought to do. Christmas was almost upon us and there was talk of our unit moving away from Singapore in the near future. I decided to put off seeing Anna until we were given the full details. We were then advised that Java was to be our next destination. We had all heard a great deal about the lovely Javanese women and we were delighted with the posting.

However, the incidence of venereal disease was known to be as high in Java as it was found to be the situation in Singapore. The Japanese had been very sexually active and had left a few problems for the British soldiers.

Immediately following being given the news that we were moving, I went to see Anna at the Toc H. As I walked in it was obvious that everybody had been waiting for me to put in another appearance, although they were aware I had been busy since our evening out. There were big smiles and waves here and there. It seemed a long walk from the door to the counter. I had an awful feeling in the pit of my stomach and wondered if I could go through with saying good-bye. Obligingly, everyone disappeared and left Anna and me to talk. Straight away Anna told me she knew my unit was being moved to Java. I was amazed as it was only a matter of hours since we had been given the news. It transpired that she had been told by a chap from our unit who was also one of her admirers. I thanked her for the evening out and asked her to pass on my regards to her father, her other relatives and friends. She asked me a lot of questions including how long I would be away, how much longer had I to serve in the army and was it possible to buy me out?

I was stunned. Never before had I given much thought to such things. I had always considered everything that happened to be a matter which was in the lap of the gods, over which one could exercise little control. It now seemed I would have to start taking life seriously. I managed to talk my way out of the difficult situation by promising to write to her as soon as I had settled in Java. I also had to agree to go straight round to her place upon my return to Singapore. Whether it would have been possible to avoid being seen when I returned, I very much doubted.

I went back to my billet a rather mixed-up young man. As part of the advance party, I had a busy evening packing my gear. The following morning we boarded the same ship on which we had sailed a few days previously. We sailed about two hours later and watched with interest as Singapore receded into the distance. A lot had happened there in scarcely two months.

We found the snakes in southeast Asia quite fascinating. One morning on the ship, we were called to the deck to see what must have been thousands of multi-coloured snakes wriggling in the sea. I had not seen so many snakes together before or with so many different colours. The ship had to slow down and it took a long time sailing through them all. I would not have liked being shipwrecked with these creatures in the water. We established a fairly good rough guide for snakes. Constrictors were of medium length, fat and attractively coloured and not of any great concern. If, however, they were thin in relation to their length, they were poisonous and to be avoided. A cobra had a strike equal to three times the length it reared up and should it rear up to a height of six feet it was time to move very quickly indeed. That would be a king cobra which would attack without any mercy.

The distance from Singapore to Java was approximately twelve hundred miles. We took about three days to get to Batavia, a place we got to know very well. We were being sent to Java to help the Dutch with their problems with the Indonesians. During the time we were there we were paid both by the Dutch and the British governments, which was a welcome bonus. As the ship entered the dock we were all on deck curious to see if any other forces had been sent to help. We saw an Indian Division, which we had not previously seen, but they were in the process of leaving the island. Also on the dockside were a number of Japanese soldiers who did not look as if they were prisoners. We were later informed that they were to be seconded to our brigade together with some of their medical staff. It seemed strange that only a few days before we had been chasing the Japanese off the islands and now their kin were being welcomed to join our ranks. I was completely at a loss to understand the logic of how these decisions were made.

We disembarked from the ship and were given a meal on the dockside by the Army Catering Corps. The meal included the local fruit which has a rather rude shape, and I found it to be very sweet and delicious. The Japanese soldiers were fed at the same time. These were massive men standing some 6 feet, 6 inches high and, we were told, were formerly members of the Emperor's Guard – a special unit. I was not previously aware that the Japanese were made in these large sizes. We tried to get them to talk without any success and so we were no wiser.

From the docks we set off for the outskirts of Batavia. An empty Chinese school was taken over as our Brigade HQ. It looked very interesting as it had a football field at its centre. There were not many of us in the advance party and on the first night we, inevitably, got caught for guard duty. We were warned that the locals came out at night with the intention of having a good fight. As it became dark we heard the sounds of tom-toms, very similar to those in the Tarzan films we saw as children. We wondered who in their right minds would let the enemy know of their arrival and we had no idea what to expect when shots were fired from trees overlooking our position. Whoever fired had not much idea of their target and no damage was done. A party of four of our men was sent to reconnoitre the situation. They fired several shots after which all went quiet; it appeared the natives had returned to their homes.

There was a native village (These villages were called 'Kampongs') about two miles from our HQ. It had high walls surrounding the accommodation which was in the form of huts on legs. Two of our companies together with armoured cars and other vehicles arrived there early one morning. The place was reminiscent of the stockade which encircled the village where King Kong was captured. We stood guard at the gates as the battalion men searched the village with a fine-tooth comb. A large quantity of weapons and ammunition was collected. Some of the natives tried to make a break for it and we had to show them who was in charge using the skills we had acquired over the years. There were shots fired in the village and one of the natives was killed. He was laid over the bonnet of a jeep and taken round Batavia market to show what happened to those who chose to fight us. The locals had to be discouraged from their hostile activities.

Dr Sukarno, the leader of the Indonesians, had given weapons to the villagers but no training in how to use them in their fight against the Dutch government that we were representing. The natives were much better with agricultural activities than with fighting. Frequently, they would fire at random without any possible hope of achieving anything whatsoever. On one occasion some of us were standing outside the gates of our HQ talking to the men on guard duty when shots were fired from further down the road. We did not react since they were not firing in our direction. A couple of Dutch soldiers, however, who were nearby went down on their stomachs and started to fire away at an imaginary target. We wondered who had given them their training. The sole reason for us being there was that there were two Indonesian girls who bathed at a well, which was close by, on a daily basis and we liked to watch. Life out there was not all fun and we took every opportunity to have a laugh.

We thought ourselves to be good footballers and so we arranged a match one afternoon. As we went out onto the sports field, our sniper friend started taking pot-shots at us as he often did. We knew his limitations, so we ignored him and got on with the game. Shots ricocheted from the roofs of the surrounding buildings as play continued. Suddenly, there was a burst of fire from over the palm trees and that was the last we heard of the sniper. Some of our men on duty had gone on 'look-see' and frightened him off with a few shots. We won the game and our officer got us all together in the evening for a toast to ourselves and our absent friends. Those who had died were never ever forgotten.

With nothing better to do that evening we carried on drinking. We had adopted a big white duck as a pet and it would follow us around. It loved to come along for a drink but was soon intoxicated. It kept falling over, particularly so when some of us started marching up and down and it tried to follow behind.

At night in Java large frogs would come out and make a great deal of noise. One of our lads, also from Sheffield, could not sleep for their croaking and spent hours lashing at them with a spade. I do not think he caught that many as the noise always sounded the same. Another source of amusement was the pet monkeys that would raid our bed spaces when we went on parade and steal any cigarettes which had been left lying around. Then they would go swinging on the telephone wires and pretend to smoke. I saw one monkey peel a cucumber as easily as a banana. This is something we cannot do; I have tried.

We were sent to quieten a crowd that had gathered near the river than ran through Batavia. A crowd of approximately 4,000 was grumbling about something or other in their own language, which none of us understood. We stood there deciding how to deal with the situation when someone came up with the idea of sending for the Japanese who were currently assigned to our brigade. A small truck arrived carrying about a dozen Japanese soldiers. As they got out their sergeant shouted orders and, with bayonets fixed to their rifles, the men broke into a run and encircled the crowd. In no time at all, the protesters had broken ranks and within five minutes not one of them could be seen. The sergeant looked at me and smiled and I could not help doing the same. He then ordered his men back into the truck before giving a bow to those of us watching. The reputation of the Japanese was well known; they could be very rough and it was best to leave them well alone.

One day a British soldier was found dead in the river that flows through Batavia. His body had been nailed to a door and it looked very much like a crucifixion. He had been caught in the out-of-bounds native quarter the previous night, presumably looking for a woman, and had paid a very high price.

Those of us who played bridge were invited as guests of the local Dutch club. We were made extremely welcome and played as teams of English versus Dutch. It worked out very well with the English having a slight edge. At the end of the evening we were given an open invitation to go along at any time and spent many a pleasant evening with our Dutch friends. It had been raining one evening as we walked back from the club to our billets and we decided to walk in our bare feet. It felt great but the guard on the gate could not believe his eyes as we went by with boots in our hands.

A battalion of the Argyll and Sutherland Highlanders had arrived in Batavia before us and had got themselves good accommodation inside the city. There was always animosity between us as both battalions considered themselves to be the best. In consequence there were frequent fights but if anyone else tried to interfere we would join ranks immediately. That is the way we were.

Together with three other chaps, I was told my age group was due for discharge and we would be returning to Singapore. Shortly afterwards we said our good-byes to all our mates in the 5th Parachute Brigade and moved to some billets at the edge of the sea near the docks. We stayed here for several days which we spent on the beach. During the time we were waiting for our ship to arrive a party of Gurkha troops moved into nearby billets. The 5th Parachute Brigade was scheduled to move to another part of Java and the Gurkhas were to take over their position. We always got on well with the Gurkhas and went round to see them. They had come to Java by way of Burma and Malaya and were well versed regarding 14th Army tactics. We were invited to one of their parties and we all thoroughly enjoyed ourselves.

The day came for us to board the ship that was to take us back to Singapore. After a long time queuing, the four of us eventually found ourselves on F deck – just on the waterline. It was not my first choice but the chances of being torpedoed now were slight and so it did not really matter. The army officer responsible for getting the troops on board tried hard to get the people with monkeys to leave them behind. Threats that they would be thrown overboard if later found seemed to have little effect.

We left Java some time in the afternoon. My three friends and I were detailed for picket duty in the evening. The weather took a turn for the worse during the period of our watch with gale force winds and torrential rain. Safety ropes were placed around the deck so that we had something to hold on to when patrolling. One of the naval officers told us that we were caught in the tail of a typhoon that was causing chaos around Sumatra and the islands to the west. Many of the ship's passengers were sick but my mates and I were all OK. We spent most of our time on duty making sure that the men who were being sick did not fall overboard. What a night it was.

It was still very rough the following morning with waves sweeping completely over the ship. The Captain spoke over the Tannoy system and said everything was OK but that we had been blown over one hundred miles off course. Gradually, the weather eased and the rest of the trip was reasonably pleasant. My thoughts turned to what I should do when we were back in Singapore. Should I make myself known or keep in the background? As Singapore came into view on the horizon the memories came flooding back. When the Cathay building could be seen I was almost in a panic.

Shortly before landing we learned that there had been a purge on the men who had taken their pet monkeys on board. Apparently naval officers had thrown them overboard leaving them a long way to swim back to dry land. Their owners had been warned.

Coming ashore I wondered if any of the Chinese would recognise me and pass the word along. I then thought that it was ridiculous to worry unduly. Had I done anything wrong? Was it not my own business?

We were taken outside the city to a large transit camp where we stayed for a couple of days before joining the troopship *Dunera*. I just had time to go into Singapore to buy some presents. It was the time of the Chinese Christmas which was being celebrated with a great many fire crackers. This Christmas they had something to celebrate of course – the removal of the Japanese.

On the ship I was again allocated F deck. On board were the men who had finished their time with the army overseas. Most of them had been in Malaya, Singapore or Burma. Very little happened on the way home. There were the usual bets on how far the ship travelled in 24 hours; I never knew anyone who had won this bet. We crossed the Indian Ocean, picked up small groups of men from Aden and Somalia and called in to Tripoli which was also full of memories. It seemed a long time since the Victory Parade in 1943. Gibraltar came into view briefly then disappeared in the haze. From the Bay of Biscay to the docks in Glasgow the weather was poor.

From the docks we were taken to a camp where men were being put through the process of being demobilised from the army. A long line of men went through seemingly endless sheds and were given a new suit, a pair of shoes, a raincoat and a trilby; they were also paid any money due to them. It was an involved job with all the various sizes of clothing that were required, but it was completed in one morning. We were given a quick meal and then taken to the local railway station where I caught a train back home to Sheffield. It was all over so very quickly. After giving our services to the war effort over many years it seemed the authorities could not get rid of us quickly enough.

18

Civvy Street Blues

During the first few days as a civilian I had rather mixed feelings. Everything was entirely different from being in the army. I could please myself what I did and when. I gave my paratrooper's red beret to my mother and she was delighted. All my friends were pleased to see me, particularly Irene, my girlfriend. Some time ago, we had arranged to get married when the war was over and preparations for the wedding were soon under way. However, my first priority was to get employment. It was far from easy. The war in Europe had finished almost twelve months previously and most of the men who had left the army at that time had got jobs. Those, like myself, who came out later found obtaining work to be extremely difficult.

I quickly realised that being in the army had not provided me with any worthwhile qualifications for being employed as a civilian. No one seemed to have a vacancy for an ex-paratrooper who had expertise with revolvers, rifles and machine guns and could also read Morse code sent in several ways. I went all round Sheffield looking for work as a driver of a van, lorry or bus but most employers seemed to think ex-servicemen were only useful for driving tanks. Those who were in work hardly wanted to know you since you were a person who might take their job. The days of 'Welcome Home' for those leaving the forces were over by the time I was discharged.

Eventually, I was given a job at the local steel firm of Daniel Doncaster. They employed me as a trainee 'back tongsman' working on a three-ton forging hammer. It was hard work and my hands soon got into a terrible state with their frequent cracking and bleeding. I found it painful even to light a cigarette. A worker who had been in the industry for many years then advised me to urinate on my hands on a regular basis. This I did and my hands became as hard as the steel with which we worked.

As I settled down at the steelworks, Irene was very busy with preparations for our forthcoming wedding. She really set about the job in earnest and I was proud of her. Her parents were publicans and she helped with the running of their pub. When my shift at the steelworks permitted, I would also help with the serving of customers and other jobs such as dealing with some awkward people.

Working in the foundry was a thirsty business and the men on the hammers did not have an ounce of fat on their bodies. At the end of an eight-hour shift, depending on the time of day, we would go to a hostelry in Dixon Lane. The first pint we never tasted but the second was very enjoyable. After that you either carried on and had a few more or you were a good lad and went home to your wife if you had one. Not an easy decision and not everyone was good – woe betide them.

1946 was a time of rationing and there was a beer shortage. A public house would open its doors and be immediately swamped by men who drank all the beer available very quickly. Another pub would then be sought. It was quite a game finding one that was open. Men would stand on street corners and signal to others when one opened its doors. At Irene's father's place, where I helped, we would be rushed off our feet for an hour or so and then we would have to close until the next day. Each public house was given an allocation based on the quantity it sold pre-war. This led to difficulties as the demand for beer appeared to be greater than previously. Landlords tried to look after their regular customers and strangers were not always made welcome.

As the date of the wedding drew closer, Irene and I were required to visit the vicar each week for advice, and the banns were read in church. I had a new suit made which required several visits to the tailor to ensure it was a good fit. It all took up at lot of time and I had not previously appreciated that getting married was so complicated. At work I was promoted to the position of 'front leverman' which included the responsibility of seeing that the furnaccs were operating correctly. I received a lot of help from the man in charge with tips on how to approach various jobs.

August 1946 arrived and the date of our wedding. My 'stag' night included friends, drink and a good old singsong. I was joined by my best man, Duncan Robertson, who travelled down from Stranraer in Scotland. He was with me in the 5th Parachute Brigade. We were married at St John's in Ranmoor. It is a lovely church just off the Fulwood Road on the outskirts off Sheffield. The service had been set for 10 o'clock in the morning and, after a hectic evening the night before, it was a rush to get ready for the ceremony. The weather was kind to us with a lovely fine day. I remember standing in the church with my best man waiting for Irene and her father to arrive and feeling very proud that everything was going so well. When the music suddenly went louder I sneaked a quick look over my shoulder to see them coming up the aisle. After the service we were taken to the vestry for the completion of the paperwork and then it was the time for the photographs with the usual instructions to stand here, there and everywhere.

The reception was held at Irene's father's public house. Irene's mother had done an excellent job of the catering. With food still being rationed, friends and neighbours had rallied round and given some of their coupons so that we could have a cake made. The meal was first class – particularly so in view of the shortages which existed at the time. After the speeches and much well-wishing, Irene and I went by taxi to the railway station where we caught the train to London for the first part of our journey to Bournemouth. As we made our way, with our luggage, to the taxi rank at Kings Cross, Irene broke a suspender. Once in the taxi, she rummaged through her handbag for a safety pin and was very relieved to have completed the repair before we reached the railway station. I thought it was most amusing, although she was a little embarrassed.

We reached our hotel in Bournemouth in the evening. It was owned by a cousin of mine and she made us very welcome. Her mother was my Aunt Rose who, together with her husband, was living at the hotel while looking for a house in Bournemouth. I had several other relatives in the area and I took the opportunity of introducing Irene to them during our honeymoon. Top of our list was a cousin who was a musician. Before the war he played the trumpet in a band that entertained on the houseboats that sailed on the River Thames. He was good company and an excellent player. His rendition of the 'Flight of the Bumble Bee' was wonderful. We returned to Sheffield having had a very good time.

Returning to work was not so easy although I soon got back into the routine. I was working at Ponds Forge in a first-class team and earning good money. Shortly before Christmas, Irene told me she was pregnant. We were both delighted with the news. This was our first Christmas together and we decided to make it one we would remember. Irene had many relatives including parents, six uncles, six aunts, numerous cousins and a grandmother. They all turned out in force on Christmas Day and we had a really memorable time. It was certainly better than the previous Christmas that I had spent in Batavia.

With the arrival of 1947, I was finding it increasingly difficult to settle down to the routine of civilian life. After a hectic time in the army, I often found life to be dull and unexciting. Irene and I spent many hours discussing our problems. We realised we had a lot of things going for us but we both recognised that we were a little frustrated. Clearly this was not a good thing for a newly married couple with a baby on the way. Some sound advice would have been welcome. I do not think we could have tried harder to settle than we did.

Irene was taken into a nursing home to have our baby and after a troubled night our daughter weighed in at six pounds, five ounces at 3 o'clock in the morning. We were all over the moon including the customers of the public house. The weather was very cold and there was a fair amount of snow on the ground. The doctor assured me that everything was all right with Irene and the baby. He also looked well in his demob suit. The snow was still with us when I fetched Irene out of the nursing home with our baby whom we had by now named Jennifer.

At the foundry I was involved in an accident. Our hammer crew was turning over some half-ton ingots in the furnace when one slipped and hit me under the chin. I did not see a doctor but had to live on what we call 'pobs' – bread and milk – for the next month. It was not very sustaining but I managed.

My difficulties in coping with civilian life continued to be a major problem. I really tried hard to come to terms with my life but I found it to be impossible. To make matters worse, the people who mattered to me could not see why I was so frustrated. One Saturday morning, Irene and I were shopping in Pinstone Street when we met an ex-Para mate and his wife. They were both pleased to see us and it soon became clear they had been going through the same sort of agonising as we were. He had decided it would be best to go back into the forces in an attempt to get it out of his system.

Irene and I had not considered this as an answer to our problem. Neither had we realised that other ex-servicemen were also having difficulties in settling down. My friend had re-enlisted in order to complete twelve years with the Colours, of which he had two years to serve. This was about the same period as myself. It was clearly necessary for Irene and myself to sort out our troubles as quickly and as amicably as possible. After a great deal of thought and discussion, and a little crying, we decided that I would also return to the army for two years in an attempt to resolve matters one way or another.

The decision having been made, I went along to the local recruiting centre and completed the paperwork. An officer told me that several ex-infantry men had joined the Signals and I elected to do the same. A medical examination passed me A1 and a few days later I received a rail pass to take me to the Royal Corps of Signals at Pocklington airfield in Yorkshire.

19

Return to the Army

A t the Pocklington camp there were several men I had
known from my previous time in the forces. They had also
experienced difficulties in civilian life but were not sure that
they had done the right thing by returning to the army. It was
now too late for changing our minds. There were several other
units spread around the airfield; these included RASC and
RAOC. Basically, it was a camp where initial training was done
before men were posted to other units in the UK and overseas.

The first two months were spent with drilling and various
exercises. My experience with map reading proved useful and
I was given the task of teaching the subject. I was drafted into
the 22nd Guards Brigade but made an application for a parachute refresher course, in case it was possible to rejoin my old
unit which was in Palestine at the time. It was approved and
I went through the routine of three daylight jumps from a
plane and one night drop from a balloon.

I was then transferred to Canterbury. Married quarters were
available and my request for accommodation was granted at
the first attempt. Several of my friends helped me to scrub out
the place and generally give it a face lift. By the time Irene
and young Jennifer arrived the quarters were looking very smart
and shipshape. The evening of their arrival we went to the
Singing Kettle, a hostelry popular with the military, where we
had a very good supper. It was a very pleasant occasion that
we still talk about even today. The few months that Irene,
Jennifer and I spent in Canterbury were very happy times. We
had a lot of fun sailing on the river with me doing my best to

compete with the local University teams. As one team passed us, I would take on the next. The weather was kind and we had some excellent picnics on the river bank. After chasing the cows away, we would settle down and enjoy the afternoon playing with our daughter. Like all good times it had to end; my unit was posted to Malaya. I had to take Irene and Jennifer back home to Sheffield where they were to stay with Irene's parents until I came back to the UK. This was not a good time for any one of us.

When I returned from Sheffield, my unit transferred to Purbright where the Guards had a large rifle range and where we all got together as a brigade before moving overseas. It was 1948 – the year England hosted the Olympic Games. We then moved to Dover and met up with other Guards battalions before embarking onto the ship. I was allocated a hammock on F deck once again. No surprise here. After settling in our new quarters, we went on the deck for a final look at the dockside. A band was doing its best to give us a sentimental send-off as the ship began to move away. It was very emotional and, not being keen on good-byes, I retired down below.

The first few days at sea were spent finding our way around. Daytime activities included physical training, map reading, weapon training and sports competitions. In the evenings there would be 'Housey-Housey' or we would play cards. The distance the ship travelled each day seemed to be a good source of income for the ship's officers and no one else. Our role in the lottery was to pay up and look pleasant. We, the 'odds and sods' troops, blended in reasonably well with the Guardsmen. It seemed the main asset of the Guards was a loud voice and, of course, big feet.

We travelled through the Mediterranean and down the Suez Canal where we had the usual bum boat attached to the side of the ship. These boats were manned by Arabs who would first travel the Red Sea one way and then return from whence they came, courtesy of another ship. Turning away from Africa, we headed for the Indian Ocean and it grew extremely hot as we approached the Equator. We then called in at the port of Colombo and were disappointed not to be able to buy a decent pint of beer.

While we were ashore in Colombo we became friendly with a group of sailors whose ship was in dry dock and they took us on board in the evening. The Master at Arms caught us drinking and generally making merry in the ship's mess which was not permitted. He chased us all over the frigate, up and down companionways and into the cinema. We tried to disappear but he was too good for us. He had the gangways removed to prevent our escape but he had obviously not met our type before. It was a long drop from the deck on to the quayside but we all made it safely. We heard instructions had been issued for us to be picked up by naval patrols and so we went first for a haircut and then a good meal. The patrols were looking for men who were drunk, not those who had signed the pledge – if only temporarily.

The ship left Colombo and headed south-east down by Penang in Malaya. Not long after we sailed there was a commotion on the deck. A large snake had been spotted in the water and the men thought it was a sea serpent until I informed them it was, in fact, a python. They could not believe snakes of that size would be seen in Malaya. From that time, I was regarded as an expert as far as reptiles were concerned and was frequently questioned on the subject. As we entered the docks in Singapore, my thoughts were of my previous visit which did not seem to be so long ago. I also thought of Irene and Jennifer and the need to sort myself out in the forthcoming months. Being married had already been helpful in having an impact on the way I conducted myself. I now carefully studied a situation before rushing in head first as was the case previously.

The brigade moved into a camp on the outskirts of Singapore and those of us who were classed as Signals were soon dashing about making contact with other units on the island. We were equipped with new motor transport and the Signals alone were provided with over sixty vehicles. The Guards battalions, comprising one Battalion of each Regiment of the Coldstreams, the Scots and the Grenadiers, held a big parade in Singapore which, I understand, was to make the local population aware of who was in charge. We then moved to Kuala Lumpur with the majority travelling by train. The railway station in Singapore was very busy with organised chaos reigning supreme. As our train departed, more soldiers awaited the arrival of the next.

In the train I was in an upper bunk by the door connecting the carriages. There was an electric fan above my head for which I was grateful with Malaya being as warm at night as it was during the day. As we passed along the causeway which connects Singapore Island with Malaya the train was boarded by Customs officials but they made no inspections in the carriages carrying the military personnel. It seemed an obvious way of smuggling goods into Malaya.

There were armed Malayan troops guarding the front and rear of the train but, since we did not run into any trouble, we did not have the opportunity of seeing them in action. We arrived at the main railway station in Kuala Lumpur and were taken to our new camp which was in a big park at one side of the University. It was called Coronation Park and was bounded on one side by the local Prison where the Malayans carried out the death sentence by hanging. Nearby there was a large Chinese housing estate and also an extensive industrial complex.

Our accommodation comprised tents under very large *attap* roofs with open sides – the roofs keeping out the rain. We quickly organised the facilities for cooking and the storage of food. The toilets were located on some rough ground facing our billets and were built of galvanised sheets bolted together in a line of about twenty or so. Each morning, I was always up early and would make it my practice to run a big stick along the rear of the sheets and make a horrendous noise. As I have previously stated, snakes tend to congregate in toilets during the hours of darkness but do not like to be subjected to noise and vibrations. The sight of the snakes moving out of the toilets at speed was most interesting. The first time I did this, the snakes swiftly moved over to our tents where some men were still sleeping. I watched, at a distance, the activity of men jumping on to their beds in an attempt to get out of the path of the terrified snakes. Experience had taught me something although I still did not know how a tourniquet was placed on one's backside.

At night time, when you were in bed, you could hear the snakes chasing rats. There was always a great deal of activity in the monsoon drains which were about two or three feet deep. First there would be much squeaking and then an ominous silence. It appeared the snakes would inject a large quantity of venom into the rats to knock them out, returning later to swallow them whole. The Guards battalions settled down to their job of keeping control of the local terrorists. The Scots Guards were stationed near one of the rubber plantations, Batu Arang, and had some trouble with the local rubber tappers who were of Indian nationality. According to a story in the local newspaper, the Guards had shot a few thinking them to be communists. I tried to find out the truth during my visits around the battalions but nobody was prepared to speak on the matter. It seemed someone, somewhere had made a mistake but the details remained elusive.

Weightlifting was an interest of mine and while I was at the base camp in Coronation Park, I formed a training class which met on three evenings per week. I could 'curl' my own body-weight at any time and the other men who joined found their physique improved considerably. The Ceylonese also had two weightlifting teams and they would compete with us at regular intervals. It was great fun.

Sometimes I would be put in charge of an armoured car which carried ten men and escorted a convoy as far north as a place called Mentakab. There was not much there – only one street with a few huts on either side. We had some Gurkhas stationed there and we kept in touch. We usually would take about a dozen primed hand grenades with us on these journeys in case we ran into trouble. Any not used were made safe on our return and stored for the next trip. On our way back to camp the smell of the fish market in Kuala Lumpur could be sensed from about three miles away. Some shops would gut the fish and then lay them in the sun to dry off. It was a really strong smell.

Kuala Lumpur was an interesting place that I took every opportunity to wander around when not on duty. I watched carpenters making big Chinese coffins and asked them if they would make one for me. When they told me the price I decided to defer the purchase for the time being since there was no way I could afford to go into their Kingdom of Heaven. I would have to rely on the state to bury me.

When these Chinese carpenters took time off for a bite to eat I would sometimes join them for a chat. We got on well and some could speak passable English. We used to go into a cafe that was near their workplace and they would, generously, share their food with me. I would do odd labouring jobs while they worked. They did not understand why I was so interested in their work but were very tolerant of my presence. I wanted to learn and did my best to explain that this was my only reason for being there.

I saw several Chinese funeral processions, making their way to mausoleums on the outskirts of the city, during my time in Kuala Lumpur. A Chinese person would have no expense spared for his or her funeral. First, there would be the massive coffin on a large hearse with curtains hung round. A number of women dressed in black would be holding onto the sides of the vehicle: these were known as 'paid mourners'. The relatives would follow on foot after the hearse. It appeared that the oldest took precedence and the remainder followed in age order with the children bringing up the rear. Following the relatives would be a band, more people and then, perhaps, another band. I saw funerals that had as many as eight bands in attendance, sometimes all playing different tunes – or so it seemed. To see the relatives and other mourners laughing and joking it would appear they were all enjoying a glorious day out together. The Chinese are a very superstitious race and frequently laugh and look happy to ward off evil spirits. I think this may have been the reason for all the merriment. My interest in these ceremonies meant I watched several, but none of the Chinese were at all disturbed by my presence.

The responsibility of organising sports days was placed in my hands. I was told if successful they would be a monthly event. Six men were made available to me and I was authorised to draw whatever was needed from the stores at area HQ. I was not all that keen on sport at that time but was determined to make the first meeting an event to remember. A sports field was selected and for a solid month I supervised the setting-out of the tracks for every conceivable field and track event – not forgetting the javelin, which I hoped to win. Neither did I forget a large marquee in which we could have a few drinks. The electricians were pressed into setting up a loudspeaker system and our major was informed that the announcements were to be his responsibility. A platform was erected for the presentation of prizes by another of our officers.

Nothing was left to chance and when the day came, there was not an event I had not allowed for and not one for which we did not have volunteers to compete. Everything went extremely well. The weather was, of course, not a worry. As to the timing of the events they could not have been bettered and everyone enjoyed the beer and food we had laid on. The one disappointment came in the javelin event. A big young chap from the Coldstream Guards beat me into second place. He was about six feet, six inches tall and built accordingly – hard luck for yours truly. A good report was received from area headquarters and as promised the sports day became a monthly fixture.

I then returned to escort duty with the convoys going up to the north. As we went out of Kuala Lumpur we could see a number of the Chinese were giving us sly looks. We suspected the local communists would have been notified that we were on our way and be waiting for us as we passed through a cutting. Our Bren guns were checked in case they were needed. The roads in Malaya ran through many cuttings and the high ground at either side was a favourite place from which the communists liked to attack by firing down on us. There was not much in the way of protection and our usual procedure was to accelerate and hope for the best. It was successful most times but occasionally we had problems. The enemy disliked meeting face to face although they never got very far with their campaign of trying to take over the country.

One night, after travelling all day, we came to a British Army camp at the side of a big river which, I believe, was called the River Slim. We were provided with tents which we erected and we then settled down for the night with our feet facing the tent pole. During the night one of our lads needed to pay a call and, as I was awake, I found a torch to show him the way so as to avoid the men who were sound asleep. Wrapped around the tent pole was a snake about six feet long and yellow in colour. This was the first time I had seen a snake with this colouring. The creature kept very still and I gently woke everybody up and got them out of the tent as quickly as possible. Grabbing my *Panga* knife, which was extremely sharp, I then removed the snake's head with a single stroke. Some men had a fire going in a stockade nearby and the head of the snake was thrown on to the embers.

The men who had the fire were Ceylonese and they had not seen a snake of that type before. It is important the head is destroyed because the venom is retained in the sacs and it can still kill you, should you happen to tread on it and release its contents. When I first came to Malaya, I met a rubber planter who had been on the island for over fifteen years and had never seen a snake. Whether the amount of drink he consumed had anything to do with it is a matter of debate. I had seen more than enough for both of us.

The army units that went into the Malayan jungle in search of the communists used *Dyak* hunters as guides. *Dyaks* were originally head hunters many years ago. They were generally fearless but most of them were terrified of reptiles. I became friendly with two who could handle snakes – they would pick them up by their tails, whirl them round and then hit their heads against the trunk of a tree. They almost convinced me I would be able to do the same thing and, feeling very brave, I picked up one and whirled it round, trying to keep the body of the snake at full length. It tried to get back at me and I finished up slinging it as far away as I could. I was terrified and it was a long time before I repeated the exercise. The *Dyaks* thought this was great fun and had competitions to see who could throw the snakes the farthest distance. I had not lost face with the *Dyaks* but all our lads thought I was completely crazy. The *Dyaks* were also good at tattooing. They would sit around a fire and burn sticks until they were like needles and then press them into a man's arm, making an attractive design of some sort. Many of the lads had this done but not me: I could imagine what Irene would say if I arrived home with tattoos on my arms.

When we were in the jungle, we would watch the *Dyaks* pick

leaves and berries of various trees and eat them. We then knew it was safe for us to eat the same things and that way we never suffered from hunger for any length of time. There is more to living off the land than you think when you first try it in the jungle.

We had been in the jungle for several weeks and when we came out, we decided to camp close to a village populated by Chinese citizens. The village comprised one street with huts on both sides. On the first night we were there, the Chinese elected to get rid of the evil spirits from the village and as darkness fell they began to march up and down banging their drums as they did so. This activity continued all night long with the result we got no sleep and the next day we had many very ill-tempered men. We resolved never to pitch our camp near a Chinese village again. We caught some communists that day and they bore the brunt of our feelings. They had tried to steal food from a village near our camp and a Gurkha patrol had run across them when returning to our base.

For the next few weeks we were concerned with keeping the battalions in touch with each other. The Grenadiers were having trouble with occasional attacks by guerrillas as they policed the area, but the main cause of concern was to the north of Kuala Lumpur. I was having problems with internal haemorrhoids and, after a short wait, I was instructed to report to the hospital in the south of Kuala Lumpur. This hospital was well laid out with all buildings being of single storey construction and with covered interconnecting walkways.

The nurse in charge of the ward was also from Sheffield and so we had plenty to talk and joke about, including my forthcoming operation that he described in great detail. If he thought it would have any effect on me he was mistaken. I was not given to worrying about such matters. In the operating theatre I was placed on a form only six inches wide and my feet were placed in slings which, I was told, would be drawn over a beam in such a manner as to allow the surgeon access for the operation. The anaesthetist came into the theatre and informed me that ether was no longer being used and a new drug, Pentathol, would put me to sleep. It worked very quickly and I came round with my nursing friend from Sheffield pretending to be surprised that I was still in the land of the living. After a few days in hospital the nursing staff attempted to remove the drainage tube but it had become stuck with dried blood. They eventually got it out but not without a great deal of effort on their part and excruciating pain on mine. The rails of the bed became twisted as I held on to them during the removal of the tube. I then found it was not possible to go to the toilet properly – it seemed as if I were constipated. For three days I tried hot baths before getting relief, and then the cause of the problem came to a light – a swab had been left inside me. I cleaned myself up, wrung out the swab and stormed into the doctor's office without knocking. Slapping the swab on the doctor's desk, I said, 'That's the reason I haven't been able to go. You are supposed to count the swabs used in an operation, in order to avoid this sort of thing.' His response was to laugh and then call in his staff to share the joke. Everyone thought it was highly amusing except me and I was absolutely livid. For a couple of days I did not talk to anyone, I was so annoyed, but eventually, I gave in and accepted a 'peace offering' drink from the surgeon, admitting it was all a bit funny.

Ten days later I was back at my unit just in time to prepare for the next set of games which included football, tennis, badminton and boxing. In Malaya it was possible to play badminton outdoors as there was rarely any wind. We had men from various units use our facilities and they all thought the games had been well organised.

I also received the news from home that Irene had given birth to our second daughter and they were both fit and well.

We later named her Elizabeth and I regretted deeply that it had not been possible to be in the UK at the time she was born.

Our commanding officer then informed me that I would be in charge of a squad of twelve men going to the arms base in Singapore. We were to take various damaged arms from the brigade and bring new arms back to Kuala Lumpur. Several days later we set off by rail. I had told the men that I would not tolerate any trouble and anyone who stepped out of line would end up in Changhi Jail. I would personally see to that without any delay. We shared a carriage near the front of the train with some sailors from Penang who were travelling to a naval base near Johore. Several of the sailors were seriously interested in weightlifting and, as a few of us were also keen on the sport, we said we would try and meet up in Singapore where they had a forthcoming contest with a Chinese team. They got off the train at Johore and we went on to the main station in Singapore.

After leaving the train, we went to the barracks where we would be staying for two nights, then went out in the evening to the *Great World Leisure Centre* in Singapore. Here they were having a Thai boxing evening where boxers used feet instead of fists. It was all right but not quite to our liking. Then it was a few bottles of Tiger beer which always gave me a headache, this time being no exception. About 11 o'clock we had a good supper back at the barracks – something that was not possible in Kuala Lumpur. The men stationed here certainly enjoyed themselves and when someone mentioned chasing communists they had not the foggiest idea what you were talking about. Some did the job and others watched.

Early the next morning we were on our way to the arms depot. The base was very security conscious but one section was losing articles on a regular basis. Omega watches were been stolen from a store almost in the centre of the camp and no one could establish just how they were taken out through the high security controls. One day a jeep was carrying two military policemen on the perimeter road outside the camp and they saw an old Chinese man sitting on a box alongside a monsoon ditch. They stopped to question him and as they did so a piece of paper, folded in the shape of a boat, came along a small stream that led from the camp into the monsoon drain. The MPs picked up the paper to find a new watch inside. Further investigation revealed the full story. Chinese workers were employed in the centre containing the watches. A stream ran under the floorboards and the watches were placed into the paper boats for collection by the old man waiting near the ditch. The authorities had no chance of recovering any of the watches. The Chinese lived near the docks, many of them on houseboats, and finding anything was virtually impossible in that rabbit warren.

In the evening, as arranged, we attended the weightlifting contest in the Chinese area of Singapore. There were crowds of people queuing to get in to the big hall and eventually, with a bit of elbowing, we managed to secure seats near the front. The lifting started with two local Chinese teams competing with each other. Both had some good strong men and it got the evening off to a good start. It was then the turn of the naval men to take on the Ceylonese team who lived locally and taught weightlifting in Singapore. The naval team just managed to pip the Ceylonese by a whisker and the Chinese cheered like the very devils they tried so hard to avoid. The captain of the naval team introduced us as an army team and we filed onto the platform to give a little exhibition to round off the evening. My party piece was to 'curl' my own body-weight several times in a routine: it went down very well and I was well applauded. It was a very pleasant evening that we rounded off with a drink with our new-found friends. The captain of the Ceylonese team told us he used to train at the

YWCA in Kuala Lumpur and since we had also trained there, we had plenty to talk about. Our Chinese friends owned the taxis and they insisted on taking us back to our barracks free of charge.

The following morning we collected our new arms and went straight to the station to catch the train for the long journey back to Kuala Lumpur. The other passengers on this trip were mostly Indian and we spent the evening with them playing cards. After passing through Customs control at Johore we retired to our bunks. A truck picked us up the next day at Kuala Lumpur station and took us back to our camp at Coronation Park. We handed over the arms to our armourer and were congratulated by our CO on a job well done. He had also received a good report on our behaviour from the barracks in Singapore. They were watching you wherever you went. I had already thanked my squad before arriving back in camp.

On my return, my first job was to obtain the company's laundry from the dhobis. The quartermaster had gone to the laundry only to find that all the workers were drunk and laid flat out. I smiled and said I would see to it. Previously, I had laid the law down and told them that, before they decided to get sloshed, they had to complete the washing of the 22nd Guards Brigade's clothes and put them on one side – or else they would be in serious trouble. I took a 15cwt truck and a couple of men and went off to the laundry. As we approached their compound we could hear Indian music wailing away on the only gramophone I ever saw out in Malaya. Whenever they had their drinking sessions they would play it non-stop. We went into their wooden hut and found them all flat out. When these people got drunk they were out for days rather than hours. I then went to another building where the finished laundry was kept and, sure enough, there they were, all our clean clothes properly wrapped and labelled.

The laundry workers were usually back at work after a couple of days and we would return to pay them for their services. Before handing over the cash, I went through the ritual of playing merry hell with the 'boss' man and calling him all the names under the sun. I enjoyed this pantomime. When I had exhausted my oratory we would compare records and payment would be made. He kept very good records and we always ended up having a good laugh.

One Friday evening, I was coming out of our canteen after having a few beers and sitting on the top of one of the huts was a rather large monkey. I gathered up a few stones and threw them at its head, telling it to clear off somewhere else. It looked at me, picked up the stones that had landed nearby and threw them back at me, refusing to move. I think it had done this before and it was only after enlisting the help of others from the canteen that we managed to chase the creature, which decided to disappear in the direction of the cookhouse. Judging by the shouts I heard later, the animal must have been upsetting the cooks.

Stray dogs were a quite a problem on the camp and we had as many as seven at one time. Rabies was the main concern. The police were responsible for dealing with their disposal. They would get hold of a bitch on heat and stake her out in the middle of our parade ground, to attract other dogs. A police marksman, an excellent shot, then proceeded to pick them off one by one. Not everyone liked seeing this happen but chances could not be taken with rabies.

The police were also having trouble with a crocodile on the river as it flowed into Kuala Lumpur. They suggested I went along to watch their attempts to get rid of the menace. The local paper carried an article about a Chinese man who had been attacked by a crocodile and had lost two arms and one leg as a result. I was late getting to the location of the police operation and they had got the crocodile cornered by the time I arrived. However, it looked as if I would be in at the kill and be able to relate the tale to my grandchildren. There was a great commotion as men dashed around and the crocodile angrily moved about, snapping its jaws. The creature was on the bank, thrashing its tail in all directions and flattening everything in its path. Shots were fired and it seemed the crocodile was wounded. That did not help matters and, if anything, made the situation even more dangerous. A further shot and all went quiet. It jerked once and no more. Cautiously, the police approached the body and after a tense few moments the cry went up that it was dead. Everyone watching gave a big cheer – it was a great feeling. The body was hoisted by a crane on to a police truck with its jaws over the bonnet, its body over the cab and its tail dragging on the ground behind. I was told it measured twenty-six feet long. The police drove their truck around Kuala Lumpur to show off their kill to the public. They deserved the respect of everyone. It takes much courage to corner one of those creatures. Another creature I came across in Malaya was the iguana. When I first saw it I thought it had been run over. As I got closer, I saw it had long front legs and short scaly legs at the rear. It was slightly taller than me, had black eyes and looked very intelligent. Suddenly, it swung its tail and went off at an astonishing speed. There was no way I could have kept up with it as it darted into the woodland.

In the evenings after dark we hung hurricane lamps on the framework outside the tents. The lights attracted big moths measuring as much as twenty inches from one wing tip to the other. We measured them and the shadows they made looked unbelievable. Malaya certainly had some strange creatures.

There were times when nothing unusual happened and the routine of army life seemed humdrum and boring. Then, suddenly, everything turned upside down when something unexpected occurred. One morning, I was on my way to the local hospital in a jeep that was being driven by a young soldier. As we were going through the local native quarter, with its countless cyclists, all with their own idea of the Highway Code, a Chinaman came straight at our vehicle. The young driver had no chance whatsoever. The Chinaman had cracked his skull and was dead. I expected trouble and sent the driver to the hospital with instructions to bring an army ambulance back. I waited with the body and did my best to keep the curious natives at bay. What a job that was. Local ambulance crews would not carry dead bodies in their vehicles – what happened in such circumstances I do not know. One thing I did know was that this dead body was going to be taken to the local police station, even if I had to carry it myself.

The driver went off and I dragged the body to the side of the road and then cleared the area of the sightseers. The locals did not like my rough tongue though they backed away. It was difficult holding them back for over an hour but I kept at it and did not show them that I was very worried indeed. Keeping a very straight face, I sent them on their way in no uncertain manner. The problem was that as one group left they would be promptly replaced by another. It was a difficult time for me and I was very relieved when the army ambulance arrived. When it had drawn to a halt, I detailed four Chinamen to carry the body into the ambulance and they were pleased to be involved in the disturbance. Off we went to the main police station where statements were taken from the driver and myself in triplicate. Two police officers inspected the jeep and tested brakes, etc. It was found to be in good order, which was just as well since I was in charge of transport for our unit. Back at camp we were questioned by our officers, as was to be expected. I was given the dubious title of 'Killer Memmott' – much to my annoyance.

I was in the canteen one evening having a drink when one of the lads rushed in and said I was wanted by Robert Robertson, our quartermaster – or Rob as he was generally known.

He had been bitten by a snake. There were two punctures on his ankle indicating fang marks. With a razor, I slashed around these marks and then sucked and spat several times. I know that I got something out of the wound because it tasted a little peculiar. After bandaging the ankle, I arranged for a driver to take us to the hospital. When we arrived, feeling very dizzy, I nearly fell over. Two orderlies came out to help us inside and I collapsed in a heap. My mouth was dry, I felt cold and could not speak. The orderlies whipped me onto a bed and a doctor gave me an injection. I passed out. When I came round the orderlies offered me a drink of tea. I tried to get out of bed but could not stand up properly and so decided to wait until feeling better.

The doctor explained how the venom had got into my bloodstream. As I had sucked at Rob's ankle the poison had got into some small ulcers in my mouth. Many people have mouth ulcers at times without necessarily having anything wrong with them and, as my wounds were open, the venom had quickly circulated. With Rob, the venom had taken longer to get round his body. Unfortunately, Rob died. The doctor explained he had passed away shortly after I had my blackout. He was given an antidote but had not responded. Heart stimulants had also not helped. I understand he did not die a pleasant death. I was shattered. He was my best mate and I really had tried to help him. Could I have done more was the question I continually asked myself. I got out of bed and asked to see my friend. Feeling absolutely wretched, I said my good-byes to him and apologised for not doing more, whatever good that did. Then I got my driver and we left the hospital. As we went over the hill we stopped and looked down on the building where so much had happened during the hours of darkness. It was now a new day and we were short of one very good bloke.

The camp was slowly coming to life when we arrived back at Coronation Park. Word had got back that Rob had died.

We were in demand to explain what had happened but we could not say a thing until we had reported to our officers. The hospital had informed them of Rob's death and they arrived a little earlier than normal from their hotel. They first asked how I felt and it was clear from their questions they knew I had had a rough time. After I had given them the details and both the driver and myself had been questioned, we were given the day off. It was the first time I had not enjoyed having a day without any duties and, after only a short period, I returned to doing my job. I kept away from the wet canteen that evening as the memories were too fresh.

Everyone paraded the next morning for the funeral. Rob's body was collected from the hospital and brought back to the camp. A line of trucks then set off with Rob leading the way. Several other NCOs and myself were the bearers and we sat around Rob's coffin trying to laugh and joke as though he was sitting alongside us. It took some doing – we had been good pals. Arriving at the cemetery, we were joined by some civilians including two women. Our men lined in two ranks and we carried the coffin up to the grave and laid it alongside. Just as the padre was about to begin the service, there was a loud noise and the sound of shots being fired from somewhere below us. Orders were issued to form in an all-round defence, which we did immediately. The only one left in the open was Rob in his coffin. When the alarm was over I went across to the grave and helped three officers and two women to get out. They tried hard to keep a straight face as they climbed out of the grave. I suppose it was not a bad idea to get them out of harm's way. The alarm proved to be a false one and we carried on with the ceremony with each man paying his last respects to Rob. He was gone but certainly not forgotten.

It was evening when we got back to our camp. Arrangements had been made to take the camp apart to make sure there were no nests of snakes around and a start on that exercise was made the following day. It was my opinion that the snake that killed Rob was just passing through. I had seen a *krait* at odd times that had a backbone standing proud above its body. It appeared to be just going through the camp. At that time there was no antidote for the poison from this type of snake. By lunchtime the next day we had transferred almost half the stores to new areas but nothing had been found. We then concentrated on the monsoon drains where there was plenty of room for a snake to hide. During the searching we found several skins which had been shed by the snakes as they had grown larger. We were particularly anxious to find any cobras – they only had to be four hours old and four inches long to be lethal. A nest of them could have meant big trouble. If a snake discharges its venom completely it takes only four hours to replace. That is why the *Dyaks*, before they played with them, made sure the snakes had ejected their venom several times. After two days of intense activity we were satisfied that nothing had been missed.

A zoological professor came to our camp to talk to us about snakes that he had studied in depth. He stayed several days and we had many opportunities to talk. As a young student of zoology he had been interested in snakes and had often sat in a glass cage at a zoo with two king cobras. He even took a book to read inside the cage. All seemed to be going well between him and the snakes when both the reptiles turned and bit him on each leg. Immediately, he got out a large knife and sliced flesh off both his legs to stop the flow of the poison that would most surely have killed him. When I spoke to him his legs looked dreadful. He had been ill for a very long time. His advice was: never, ever trust a wild animal – they do not think like us and could turn on you at any time. The professor and I got on well and we even went snake hunting together.

I officially took over Rob's duties as acting quartermaster for the company. Part of my job was to employ civilian firms for various services such as laundry, boot and shoe repairs, tailoring and so on. It was also my responsibility to ensure that high standards were maintained by the contractors. The time came for tenders to be submitted for new contracts for the following year with Chinese and Indian firms competing against each other. Things got rather hectic and I found myself the most sought after man on the camp. Wherever I went out for an evening, there was always some representative of a company waiting to buy me a drink. After coming back to the camp several times much the worse for having too much to drink, I decided not to go out in the evening. It was a hard decision as I really enjoyed going to the Chinese quarter and watching their shows which they put on every night without charging for admission.

Sometimes, the Indian firms would call on me at the camp during the day. It got very difficult. I had a word with the officers and we had a meeting. They asked me if I was happy with the present arrangements or if I had any complaints about the service of any of the firms. I answered that everything was running smoothly and would be content for the same firms to continue. They agreed. Never change a winning team was my motto. I had done much of the running of the stores when Rob was alive and I am not an easy man to satisfy: they either did the job right or not at all. Out of all the people who worked for us, it was the people who worked hardest who received least for their efforts. The laundry workers took the trouble to take me to the cemetery to visit Rob's grave. They took me all the way there and left me at the graveside so that I could pay my respects on my own. Their boss man said, 'Rob was a good man who deserved better from life than what he had received'. I got to know these *dhobi wallahs* very well and they have hearts of gold – please do not ever run them down in my presence – they are the salt of the earth in my book.

Occasionally at the weekend we had a civilian coach to take

any men who wished to go to the coast for the day. We would spend the day swimming, eating, drinking and generally taking things easy. I was on one of these trips and cut my foot on some glass that was on the beach. A wound in Malaya can readily lead to complications and I tried to fasten a handkerchief around my foot. The Chinese do not normally go out of their way to make a fuss of the British, but a young Chinese girl who was relaxing nearby offered to bandage my wound. I accepted and you can imagine the comments from the other men as I lay on my back on the sand with this very attractive girl taking great pains in wrapping up my foot. She could speak good English and appeared to know a lot about Malaya and its troubles with the Chinese communists. It seemed the girl had done an excellent job with the bandaging and it was a pity when it was time for our coach to return to Kuala Lumpur.

I did not often report sick in the army – it was such a bind. However, I decided to do so the following morning. My turn came eventually and the bandage was removed by an orderly. Suddenly, great roars of laughter went up from the medical team as it was discovered the bandage used by the Chinese girl was made from a sanitary towel. Was my face red? I got all sorts of comments from the medical staff. It took me a very long time to live that down.

In Malaya, fever can strike very quickly. You can retire feeling quite well and wake up during the night with a raging fever. This happened to me: my head was on fire and was pounding as if it would burst. I felt very poorly and was taken to hospital in Kuala Lumpur once again. I remember very little about going into the ward. When I came round I could neither think clearly nor remember anything. The chap in the next bed told me that the drug used by the doctors was called laudanum, which was made from opium. It certainly put you into a dream-world and you were quite happy to amble along and think of nothing in particular. After a few days I was allowed to walk in the hospital's grounds. This was fine, but although free from headaches or fever, I was not getting anywhere. I went outside the confines of the hospital and sat on the grass, staring for hours on end at the traffic. Another chap, who had been stung by hornets, would sit with me and discuss absolutely nothing.

One day this other chap and I refused to have any more injections. We told the doctors that we had had enough. It was impossible to think clearly and we had no inclination even to bother to think. After much consultation among the doctors, it was decided that I would be allowed to return to my unit in a couple of days. The drug would take that amount of time to get out of my system. When I left the hospital, I queried what had been the matter with me. The answer I got was that it was NYD fever. It meant that my fever was, 'not yet diagnosed'. The doctor at our unit later told me that there were over 4,000 fevers in the Far East. Our people were only aware of the details of some 2,000 – hence the term NYD fever. No wonder I used to wander around the hospital grounds feeling like a zombie without a mind of my own.

I had been out of hospital about four days when the doctors asked me to return for a check-up to see if the drugs had got out of my system. A double tooth was giving me trouble and I thought that it would make sense to have it taken out on the same visit. The medical centre passed me as being all right and I then went along to the dental centre where the dentist examined my teeth. During the examination he told me that they had been experiencing trouble with the drug cocaine that had not been up to its normal strength lately. He gave me two injections and then I waited outside for them to take effect. When he called me in, he tapped my teeth and asked me if I could feel anything. It hurt like hell and clearly the drug was rubbish. I was offered the alternative of either having the tooth out the following morning in the operating theatre or having it out there and then without the aid of cocaine. I elected to get it over and done with immediately. It was awful but well worth the effort – no tooth and no pain.

We had over sixty vehicles and they had to be kept in tip-top condition at all times. When our major turned an ignition key the engines had to start straightaway or there would be trouble. Motorcycles had to fire at the first kick. This kept us all very busy and together with my quartermaster's duties meant I had very little free time. I did, however, occasionally get a chance in the evening to visit a Ceylonese unit that was attached to our brigade. It was only a few miles away from our camp at a place called Kelang, but to get there you had to walk through a big area of coconut groves. Walking through such a grove in the dark was quite an experience. The husks containing several coconuts always seemed to fall at night time. Since they weigh between ten and fifteen pounds, the thought of them hitting you is not at all pleasant. As you walked along you could hear them straining and starting to break off and the only sensible thing to do was to stop dead in your tracks.

When we reached the Ceylonese camp we were always made very welcome. On one occasion they were having a celebration with no expense being spared. Long trestle tables were groaning under the weight of food with all sorts of concoctions of their own making. It was a great open-air get-together with side shows and a large platform for weightlifting. The atmosphere was just great. They spoke good English – better than many of us did. As we wandered around having a good tuck-in, we came across a tent with a couple of snake charmers at work. I have seen several snake charmers over the years, but these two were taking money under false pretences. You could tell from the look of the snakes that they had no intention of coming out of their hypnotic state. I asked the charmers if it was opium the snakes had been given. The elder of the two Indians looked at me and turned away: no way was he going to talk to me – I had upset him. The chap who had invited me then came into the tent and I realised the motive for his kindness. He wanted to know how an Englishman was capable of picking up a snake and throwing it through the air. Everything went quiet and the Ceylonese man confirmed this had been a subject of conversation in the camp for the past few weeks. The *Dyaks* they could understand doing such a thing, but a Westerner was another matter. It had been my intention not to tell my story until I was about to leave for England but that was now only two months away. I promised to go back to their camp at a later date and show them how it was done. First I would see how the *Dyaks* felt about my revealing of their secrets.

The *Dyaks* were away from our camp for a few days, busy with some regiment of the Malays. The Malayans were getting ready for the time when they would run their own country and were keen to show how good they were. If nothing else, they looked tough. I did not, therefore, see the *Dyaks* before leaving for another trip around the battalions in the brigade with two other men. We enjoyed these trips and our first stop was the battalion of Grenadiers stationed at an out of the way place called Sungai Besi. There were many Chinese people in this area and I did not trust them very much. When they smiled, it did not show in their eyes. They were very different from the Chinese I knew in the Kuala Lumpur district. We spent a couple of days with the Grenadiers, giving them all the latest news, before moving on to see the Scots Guards at Batu Arang. On our way there, we had to make a call at a leper colony at a place with the name of Sungai Buloh. I was only required to deliver documents to the medical officer and so my two companions stayed in the vehicle while I went inside. They thought it was safer outside. The doctor asked how I felt about coming into the colony. I grinned and assured him that neither my men nor myself had any qualms about doing so. He said, 'Good show, I have a meal laid on for you.'

I went back to my men slightly concerned how they would react. To my surprise they both told me that it was perfectly all right and a Malayan chap with a broad smile took them off with the promise of a slap-up meal. I was hoping we would have the meal before being taken on a tour of the colony. It was more than likely I would not feel hungry if the meal came second. Fortunately, the meal took precedence and was excellent as was the company. We then toured the colony escorted by the staff. I was a little puzzled as to why we were being given so much attention. The place was very clean. Many of the staff spoke good English and seemed knowledgeable about world affairs – much more than I was. They asked how I liked the camp at Kuala Lumpur and being in Malaya. I wondered how they knew where I was stationed and was intrigued.

After seeing the patients, I was taken into the chief's office and it then became clear how these people knew so much about me. The chief was an associate of the professor who was the snake expert. We sat in easy chairs, the big man and myself, discussing a multitude of things including how I was coping with Rob's death. He asked for my opinion of the colony. I replied that I was impressed with both the organisation and the welfare afforded to his patients. Gone, for me, was the ever-present fear of catching the disease of leprosy. This man was a professor in the field and he assured me the disease was not infectious. The treatment at the colony included a medication they called *Guryun Oil*. It was taken both internally and externally and was a vegetable oil obtained from a species of fir. He was a most interesting person. A book he showed me stated that leprosy had, at one time, been a world-wide disease: it had been rife in Europe – even in England and Scotland. The Romans had supposedly carried the disease all through their Empire. It would appear the first instance of it began before 1500 BC and became established in Greece and Italy by the first century BC. I found it difficult to break off the fascinating conversation but we had to make it to Batu Arang before dark. All the staff turned out to see us off. My lads were chuffed pink that this was happening to us. It seemed that the lads had been made most welcome by the staff and addresses had been exchanged so that they could keep in touch. I must admit that the Malayan girls were very attractive, but I was married with children and that was that for me.

We made good time to Batu Arang and booked into the Guards camp. I had known one or two of the sergeants at Purbright and we were made welcome as we settled down for the night. The following day, I had a chat with the Guards quartermaster, sorting out new procedures for the stores. My men set about overhauling the engine of our vehicle. The job kept them away from the NCOs who were the most zealous I have ever met. Batu Arang was not much of a place and no one was tempted to go out and paint the town red. I had a drink with the lads that night, but as the Guards were so regimental, I put on an old shirt without any stripes and no one knew me from Adam.

Our next call was to Batu Caves. The vehicle was running much better after its 'de-coke' and after about an hour we had left the rubber estates far behind us and were enjoying the open countryside. This was an area where quite a few English families lived. They worked in government departments and in hospitals. There was one person living there whom I did not know then, but worked with in later years. She was very nice and coped with a hospital job at the same time as bringing up a family. Sister Jones did not suffer fools gladly, though in my opinion, she was the best theatre sister I have ever met.

This area was fairly high up in the hills which was the reason for its being popular with the Westerners. Batu Caves was much further down in the valleys and a great deal warmer. The driver drove a bit faster and created a little draught which we appreciated. Batu Caves were large natural caves in a hillside. In front were the huts where the men slept and big hangars where the stores were housed. This was the main centre from where all army units drew their supplies. Any change in procedures came from here: they ruled the roost.

Two days later we returned to Coronation Park. It had been an interesting few days away from the humdrum life on the camp. As we drew up inside our camp we noticed a commotion within the REME lines which were close to our own. Many of their trucks had been out with men from the Grenadier Guards and had been ambushed by the communists at the usual cutting in the hillside. We went to look and were amazed at the extent of the damage. According to the sergeant major, the trucks had been allowed to enter the cutting and were then fired on from both ends. The communists had opened up with machine guns. It was every man for himself. Firing from above, the communists had the advantage and got clean away, melting into the jungle. It was not easy fighting in someone else's backyard. We had encountered the same sort of problem in Java but there the country was flat. Here any Chinese men who assisted the British and were caught by the communists would have petrol thrown over them and be set alight.

Back home in the UK, the newspapers covered these happenings but I doubt if they ever managed to convey the feelings of the men who were directly involved. Brought up in an entirely different environment, they had to endure a much harsher side of life than that which they had been prepared for in their schooldays. They deserved a lot of praise.

Our major appointed me to give instruction to a group of Malayans in finding their way through the wild open country of the rubber estates. They seemed happy enough about it and we managed to cover a fair area to the north of Kuala Lumpur, sometimes getting very wet but never lost. We slept rough in our hammocks and everyone seemed pleased with the results.

Our new quartermaster arrived to take Rob's place. He had

come from Singapore. I was pleased as it would give me more time to concentrate on the company's vehicles. However, it was not to be. Our officers held a meeting and later informed me that they would prefer for me to continue with the job since the new chap was not familiar with the drill and had no experience of an infantry brigade. What I thought was kept to myself. From then on the new bloke did all the parades and the drilling, which suited me fine.

I was eager to see the return of the *Dyaks* and on several occasions had been to the wet canteen to check if they were back from the jungle. My concern was that they may have strayed into the Thailand jungle. Had they done so, there might have been very dire consequences if they had met up with some Thai soldiers. The *Dyaks* were a very close-knit community and thought little of other races. If you were English you were all right – if not, very doubtful. I was pleased to find they had returned when I visited the canteen one evening. They had done their job and were on their way back to Borneo. I buttonholed the two *Dyaks* with whom I got on so well and tackled them as the Ceylonese had requested. They virtually exploded and told me that should the Ceylonese come anywhere near they would throw the snakes at them and not bother removing the venom first. I backed off and did my best to remove myself from a decidedly tricky situation. From the look in their eyes I could see how they came to be called headhunters. Later I managed to take them for a farewell drink and we all ended up pals together again. They left the following morning. I did not push my luck and show the Ceylonese how the party piece was done in case my *Dyak* friends should ever return.

It was getting near the time for my return to the UK. I handed over the stores to the new quartermaster who was by now happy with what was expected of him. The vehicles were transferred to another of the sergeants and for the rest of my time I did sundry jobs as orderly sergeant. I began to be concerned about what I would do on my return home. I knew the next few months would be spent in an army depot somewhere in the UK but after that it was a matter of finding employment. My final days in Malaya seemed to drag on for a long time. I had a final chat with Rob. The major took me to see his grave for the last time but I made my own way back to camp – there were times when you needed to be alone. Coming back into the army had been right for me and I sincerely believed that I had, by then, had enough of the life for all time. I thought that another six months in storage depots would help me return to civilian life.

The lads gave me a good send-off, giving me my breakfast in bed. It was nice to hear them cheering although I suspect some had their own reasons for so doing. The journey on the train to Singapore was long and tedious. Together with an assortment of men from other regiments, I was transported to the docks where the ship, *Dunera*, was waiting. I was on my way back home to my family including the newest arrival, my daughter, Elizabeth.

20

Home Sweet Home

The *Dunera* was our home for the next few weeks. Among those who came aboard were some Ceylonese troops, although none that I recognised. It was lunchtime as we proceeded slowly one by one up the gangplank onto the ship. The sun was beating down and there was no chance of relieving my chronic thirst or having any food for a long time. After what seemed eternity, I reached the top of the gangplank and was given a card with details of where I was to sleep on the ship. It was F deck again but I was offered either a bunk or a hammock. A hammock was chosen as I expected some rough weather in the Mediterranean at that time of the year. The ship sailed the following day and headed towards Ceylon and the Indian Ocean with a group of dolphins leading the way: it was a wonderful sight.

Colombo was our first port of call and there we bought presents, walked through the market and had a meal. We next anchored at Aden for a short time, a few men embarked and we sailed away immediately afterwards. Going through the Suez Canal was an experience that does not come often in a lifetime. Watching the Arabs at work was fascinating and the decks were crowded with men giving frequent advice to the locals.

The Mediterranean was nostalgic for me. A short stay in Tripoli harbour brought back memories of the big parade during the war, when I was on guard on the rooftop of the building opposite to where the ship was moored. We did not go ashore. In the harbour, a hammerhead shark came alongside the ship. Someone from the galley threw it a French stick loaf, about two feet long, and the shark grabbed it, longways, into its mouth. I was very surprised at the width of its mouth.

As we steamed towards Gibraltar, the crew laid 'rough weather' lines on the deck. They were expecting bad weather and, surely enough, it came, with the usual long line of men on the deck feeding the fish. For a few days we had some very heavy weather and I saw a lifeboat smashed to pieces on the forward deck.

Southampton approached and everyone got their gear ready for going ashore. Over the Tannoy system orders were given regarding where the various groups were to parade and at what time. The Customs officers were waiting and from where I stood on the deck I could see how they went about their job. They did not pick out everyone – only odd ones from the queue. Those that they did select had their luggage gone over with a fine-tooth comb. Even stiff army caps were removed and examined inside. I was carrying two nice gold watches – one for Irene and another for her mother – and paying duty was something not possible out of the small amount of money I had left. Wandering around the deck, I was thinking hard about what I should do. I then saw a chap who had a very bad cold indeed. He was clearly suffering but I did not see any reason why I should not also have been inflicted with a heavy cold. I got hold of some cotton wool and placed a small piece up each nostril. A big handkerchief was wetted under a tap. I wrapped the two watches in a waterproof covering and put them into the handkerchief. Holding the package to my nose, I made my way sorrowfully along the line – my immediate companions giving me a wide berth. One of the Customs men said, 'You don't look all that happy soldier.' I walked over to him and presented him with my luggage. He could not get rid of me quickly enough.

After clearing through Customs we caught a train to Ripon

in North Yorkshire. The Royal Signals depot was two or three miles from the town centre. After settling in we were granted leave. My welcome home was marvellous. Parting and putting up with this, that and the other was over. Orders now came from my wife – *Her indoors who must be obeyed at all times.* I was under the strictest of instructions not to let the army talk me into signing on again. There was no need for her to say that – I had already decided. My leave covered the Christmas period and it was great to be back with the family.

I returned to Ripon and two weeks later was transferred to Barnard Castle – also in North Yorkshire. Here I was given the job of driving instructor. This work was shared with a sergeant who had been a Japanese prisoner of war. He was reluctant to talk and only did when it was absolutely necessary. I think he thought he was still among the Japanese. However, we got along with him looking after one half of the class and me the other. We went out in a convoy of a dozen trucks and his half led the way – which seemed to please him. We got good results.

With a month to go before my service ended, I was assigned to a job within the camp. There was no more floating out to Darlington with a convoy of trucks. It was then a case of pressure being put on me to sign on again for a further period in the army. I replied that it was time for me to call it a day. Every single day until the end of my service, I was again asked to reconsider my decision – each morning and again at 2 o'clock in the afternoon. I was offered promotion but my answer was still no. The orders from my wife were obeyed.

Had I re-enlisted it would have probably meant joining a company then being formed to go to Korea. That would have been no use at all to Irene and myself with a young family. For me it was into civvy street once again.

After a short holiday with my family, I went looking for work and, without difficulty, obtained employment in a coal mine with the name of Wharncliffe Silkstone. I was working at the coal face and from then on that was to be my way of life. The name of the pit changed a couple of times but the job was the same until I retired.

And I never touched a musical instrument ever again.